Edited by Jane E. Stahl and Susan Biebuyck
Volume Five
Printed in 2018

© 2018 Stahl/Biebuyck All rights reserved.
R. R. Bowker - US ISBN Agency
ISBN: 978-0-9788838-8-1   0-9788838-8-8

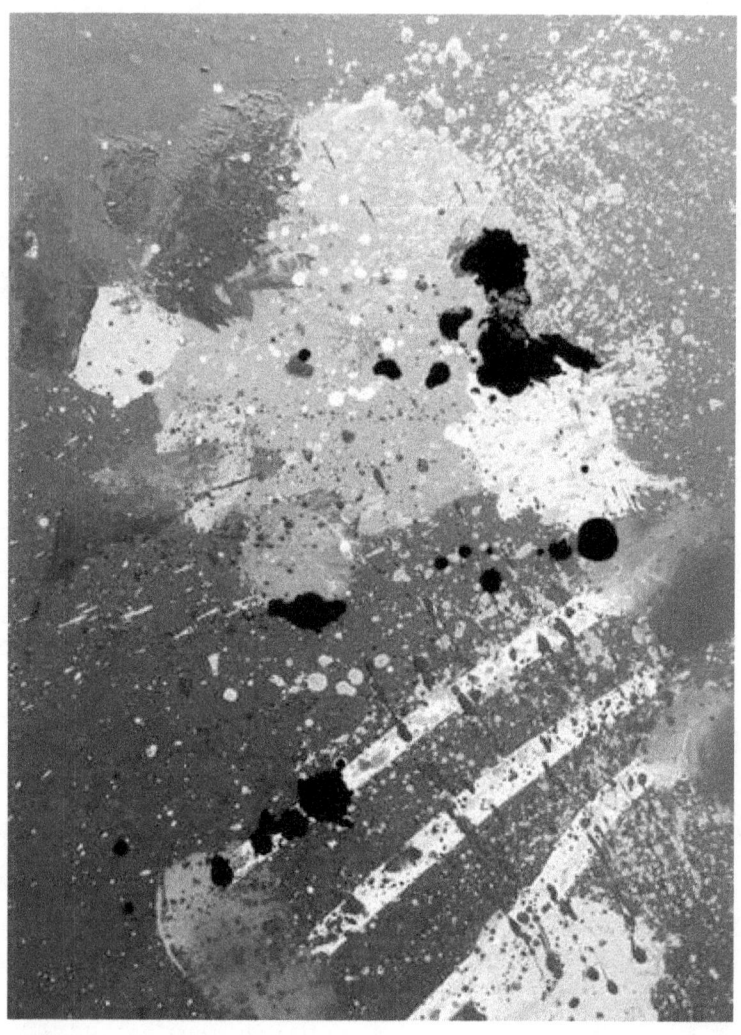

Cover art "I Heard You the First Time" by Suzanne Fellows

Preface

Let's Rant! *Challenges, Tempests, and Petty Annoyances*

Whether we're frustrated, disappointed, angry or just annoyed, the sharing of negative feelings can be cathartic, even fun and funny. Often, also, the need to release our rage overcomes inhibitions; passion overrules anxiety, and expressing these feelings—in writing or even in a public speaking forum—becomes almost effortless. My students taught me this!

We all have people in our lives who "drive us crazy," circumstances that test our patience and resolve, things that don't work or that break or make our lives more difficult than we'd like. And certainly the current social and political climate has many of us seething and seriously concerned about the future.

Such is life—full of frustrations, disappointments, and challenges—some trivial, some enormous. And while we're often encouraged not to complain, in this volume our writers have released their anger, frustration, or annoyance and have shared the "thorns" among the "roses" of their lives, the gifts in their suffering, the lessons they've learned from their trials—perhaps a piece of advice or insight for those who will follow them—or their coping style when things got tough.

On our better days these struggles can be viewed as opportunities, gifts, actually, through which we become better human beings—more humble and compassionate regarding the greater or lesser burdens of others, more appreciative of life's bounty, more obliged to ease the sufferings of others, and more joyful more often when crises abate. We become survivors.

Paul Pearsall in his book <u>The Beethoven Factor</u> suggests that some of us are not just survivors; some are thrivers, super-resilient *folks who understand that sometimes creative surrender and setting new goals is a better response than just "hanging in there." Pearsall writes of thrivers throughout human history, those who can laugh even in the midst of their pain, argue effectively against negativity and self-defeating thoughts, and find something positive to celebrate about their situation.*

To Pearsall, surviving is coping; thriving is creativity at its best. He proposed the idea that "It may be that we're never fully conscious and awake until something goes terribly wrong." He suggests that each morning we take a few deep breaths and consider why, for what, and for whom are we getting up each day. He recommends that we live each day aware of our power and our choices to create our lives—beginning with the only thing over which we have control: our own attitude.

Thus, even in the midst of whatever challenges we face, we can begin each day with the end in mind, realizing who and what in our lives is really valuable and working consciously to enhance those aspects of our lives. We can remind ourselves daily to "play the hand we're dealt," "make lemonade out of the bitterest lemons," "forgive and forget," practice perfect patience, perfect love, and divine graciousness, offering mercy above and beyond more justice whenever possible.

And while such a shift in perspective is a challenge, the shift is really as simple as changing our minds, and the reward of this shift is a lifelong serenity that is priceless. Meanwhile, as fellow recipients of life's tests of our quietude, take a peek into the tempests raging in the lives of others and know you're not alone!

Peace. Namaste. Shalom.

~ *Jane Stahl*

Curator's Preface

The art represented in this edition, our 5th "literature responding to art/art responding to literature" edition—and also the art exhibit staged at Studio B—represents a new—and especially charged—level of response.

Let me explain: at Studio B, our exhibit themes and ideas are generally created more than a year ahead. When we decided to do "Let's Rant!" as a theme, our world had entered a new era. We found ourselves in an era where art and literature had become increasingly emotionally and politically energized.

Right from the start of this era, people divided from friends, coworkers, at church or the gym. The political atmosphere forced us to find "our" places.

Some started shopping only where their preferred political party's interests were supported. On social media "Unfriending" or "Unfollowing" was at an all-time high. Even Thanksgiving had to come with rules where conversation had to be politics-free, just to get through the meal. If you didn't know your politics before, well, you sure do now.

Every image in this book was curated either for its own charge on this era or it so perfectly complemented the literature it accompanied.

Sure, there are a few politically strong pieces in this edition; but there are also pieces that cause us to reflect on our lives and humanity, pieces that enhance our ability to empathize or laugh at life's absurdity—pieces that we can all appreciate.

We proudly support both our artists and writers in this visual and complementary artistic endeavor.

~ Susan Biebuyck

Authors' Table of Contents

"All You Gotta Do" 15
   Claudia Bahorik

Trickster, Liar, Thief 19
   © 2018 *Michael Barnett*

Post-truth Discourse 21
   Virginia Beards

The Big Hype 23
   Craig H. Bennett

The Evening News 27
   Jessica Bergeman

"You're Fired" 29
   Susan Biebuyck

Dear Mr. Smith 33
   Aubrey I. Butto

#NotYouToo 35
   Patty Kline-Capaldo

Cloud Seeding 39
   Patricia D'Innocenzo

What's for Dinner? 41
   Patricia D'Innocenzo

Spotted Lanternfly 43
   Heather Goodman

Lemon Twist 45
   Sharon Hajj

Poems 1 and 2 53
   Marta Herman

iwontputonmysugarjacketdotcom 55
   jennifer hetrick

rant poem no. 17 56
   jennifer hetrick

Challenges, Tempests, and Petty Annoyances   9

YOU SAY, RANT! RANT! 59
   Annarose Ingarra-Milch

BE FEARLESS 62
   L. T. James

TO THE MAN ON THE PHONE 65
   Marilyn L.T. Klimcho

POLITICIANS 68
   Ollie Koehler

REINCARNATION 69
   Ollie Koehler

COME ON NOW 71
   Hiram Larew

SILLY 73
   Hiram Larew

ROUGE 74
   Catherine Mahony

FALL POEM 77
   Sophia Mish

AMPHIBIAN BRAIN 81
   Sylvia Morra

UNHEARD 82
   Jillian Prout

WHAT GIVES YOU THE RIGHT? 85
   Jillian Prout

DO NOT GO GENTLE INTO MENOPAUSE 89
   Ginny Rathman

POLLUTER 91
   Ginny Rathman

TAKE A KNEE 92
   Philip Repko

CAN'T 95
   Jay Ressler

STIRRING THE ASHES 97
 Martha Ressler

LOVE THEM SOCKS 99
 Dan Roberts

THE SNOW FIX 100
 Dan Roberts

MONDAY MORNING BREW 101
 Dan Roberts

OF POLTERGEIST AND ANTI-MATTER 103
 Theresa Rodriguez

REPERCUSSIONS 105
 Michael Schiffman

DISMAY AT THE GROCERY STORE 107
 Michael Schiffman

TWELVER 109
 Ron Schira

TO MY BROTHER 113
 Amy Stahl

WE ALL SUFFER THE SAME* 115
 Jane Stahl

A WISH LIST FOR OUR TIME 117
 Jane Stahl

DEATH BY APOLOGETICS 121
 J.D. Stahl

UGH! 125
 Burton Stehly

5PPM 126
 Burton Stehly

CAN I GET A WITNESS 129
 R.H. Strauss

TIRED OF BEING 133
 R.H. Strauss

THE FOUR STAGES OF A WOMAN'S LIFE EXPRESSED AS BAKERY GOODS 135
   Theodore R. Thomas
DEATH OF TRUST 137
   Theodore R. Thomas
NOT QUITE FINISHED 139
   Joanne Van Wie
THIS I KNOW 141
   Joanne Van Wie
WATCH YOUR BEST FRIENDS 143
   Diane VanDyke
OF THE MAKING OF MANY BOOKS 145
   Nelvin Vos
JAPA 149
   Sandra Williams
UNTITLED 150
   Sandra Williams
FINALLY 151
   Sandra Williams
REVENGE OF THE ANALOG 153
   Bob Wood
TONY THE LIP 159
   John Yamrus
SHE 160
   John Yamrus

Artist Index
By Order of Appearance

Cover Art "I Heard You the First Time" ......Suzanne Fellows 4
"Tech Vanitas: Black & White TV" ....Jeanette May 14
"Trump" ....Naomi Vogels................. 18
"Ya Drivin' Me Crazy!"................................Barrie Maguire 20
Digital Art "Almighty" ....Sue DaNym 22
"Words Hurt" .... Katie Hamburger 26
"Year of the Dog" ....Kathi Ember.................28
"Granny Smith" ....Susan Biebuyck 32
Poster from the march, "Pussy" ....Mary Salen...................34
"Above a Single Day"...................................Adriano Farinella...........38
"Chicken Head" .... Angela Faust-Izzo 40
"Stick a Pin in IT!" & "The Ephing SLF" .. Susan Biebuyck 42
"A Life Full of Color" ....Heather Lippincott Foust....... 46
"Be Free".. Marta Herman............... 52
"Sugar Jacket".. Susan Biebuyck 54
"Come On People!" ....Daniel Gorman................58
"Blanca" .... Sue Ciccone 63
"TechVanitas-Gray Typewriter"......................Jeanette May 64
"Biting mad!" .... Jim Meehan 68
"Butterflies Journey of Love" .... Jillian Wright-Prout...........70
"Berks View"..Lynn Millar 72
"Winter's Incipience".....................................Tamie Dickson.................74
"Sofie on the Wall" .... Matt Smith 76
"Medusa with Theater Mask" ....Reggie Waters 80
"Odds"...Lauralynn White 82

Challenges, Tempests, and Petty Annoyances 13

"Grab Pussy and Run" .... Susan Biebuyck 84
"Spot On" .... Susan Biebuyck 88
"500 years" .... Susan Biebuyck 90
"Locker Room" .... Mary Salen 96
"Snow Day" .... Ed McCarty 100
"Getting a Kick Out of Life" .... Jim Meehan 102
"99 Elephants A Day" .... Suzanne Fellows 106
"A Well-regulated Militia" .... Charley Farrell 111
"2130 Wightman St. No. 27" .... Erika Stearly 112
"Fake Art" .... Big Dutch Dave Nally 114
"Thinking Tree" .... Linda Rohrbach-Austerberry .. 117
"None of Your Damn Business" .... Charley Farrell 120
"#<3" .... Ginger Stahl 123
"Take Out - Wednesday" .... Kristen Woodward 124
"Searching for a Sign" .... Charley Farrell 128
"I Heard You the First Time" .... Suzanne Fellows 131
"Targeted" .... Sue DaNym 132
Art .... Theodore R. Thomas 134
Art .... Theodore R. Thomas 136
"Hearts and Leaves" .... Jillian Wright-Prout 138
"Me Too" .... Lauralynn White 140
"Frenchie Kisses" .... Sue DaNym 142
"Mala Beads" .... Sue DaNym 148
"Tech Vanitas: Blue Typewriter" .... Jeanette May 152
"Tamborine" .... Bob Wood 157
"Channeling Your Inner Baby" .... Jim Meehan 158

***"Tech Vanitas: Black & White TV"** photograph by Jeanette May*

"All You Gotta Do"

If I hear "All you gotta to do" again, well, I can't be held responsible! This phrase has to be the poster child's slogan for the generational gap. Really, think about this. If I really only had to do something and it were so simple or easy, I sure as hell wouldn't be asking how to do it in the first place.

Here's a perfect example. Not long ago I signed up for a course at Penn State Berks through the GO-60 program (that's what I refer to as Geezers Over 60 – one of the benefits of getting old is being able to take courses for free). But no. You just can't sign-up, pay the registration fee, and show up at class. No worry. It's simple, so they say. "All you gotta do" is followed by a list of what you gotta do.

First you need an ID. "All you gotta do" is go get your picture taken. But wait. It's summer and that doesn't apply and after several trips back and forth across campus, you find the right place, but the person isn't in. Eventually it gets done. Then you want to register your car for parking. "All you gotta do" is register it at the police station. Wrong! You have to register your car online, then proceed to the police station for the parking card. Oh, you need a handicap parking card? Another set of "all you gotta do" convoluted and unintelligible instructions, laced with multiple trips here and there across campus and to the doctor, who's never on duty.

To get email and access to the system I had to set up a bunch of accounts online and upload a photo of myself. Another "all you gotta do" project that took several phone calls, three trips to IT at the library, and help from five different people.

I'm sure there were several more "all you gotta do" steps, but eventually I made it to my class – forty years after my last undergraduate class that never required so many complicated steps (and it cost a lot less).

Not long into the semester, the instructor (still sporting his college sneakers) rolled in a cart with a bunch of boxes stacked on it. I wondered if he might be serving snacks and cocktails. Nope, wrong generation. Instead, he proudly handed out loaner I-Pads to each of us students.

"WTF?" I ask myself, wide-eyed, stroking the shining beast. Strutting around the room like Santa on steroids, the instructor informed us that we are expected to film some sort of literacy story about ourselves with the I-Pad using I-Movie.

Say what? I'm looking green because I can't even figure out how to turn the damn thing on. The girl next to me leaned over and pressed the hidden button, with a slightly conciliatory lift of her eyebrows. He's rambling on about how easy this project is, how much fun we'll have doing it, and isn't it wonderful he arranged for us to use these freaking things. I'm protesting that it's not something I can do, and he's standing there in his jeans and golf shirt telling me, "All you gotta do" to create this goddamn five minute video. Hell, I just got comfortable with Facebook and texting.

I pleaded with my teenage great nieces to help. More "all you gotta do" advice. Thanks a lot. Then, after a litany of profanity only a frustrated senior citizen could spew, I drove to Barnes and Noble, "all you gotta do" cursing all the way, and bought a forty dollar book for dummies about I-pads. Right. The book was laced with "all you gotta do" references. The goddamn book went back.

After several trips to the IT geeks, a visit in desperation to the instructor's office waving a white flag, a flood of "all you gotta do" tears, and after nearly murdering my wanna-be helpful husband, I questioned my sanity. This isn't how retirement is supposed to be. Forty stinkin' hours later I bridged the generational gap and got the SOB video done.

Point being, it's never, ever going to be a simple procedure whenever some techie snips that dreaded phrase, "All you gotta do." I warn you, just throw your hands up in surrender, scream, and do whatever it takes to make the person who said this run for cover. We oldsters should just have a sign taped to our foreheads that says, "If I hear you say, 'All You Gotta Do' you better fucking run!"

~ Claudia Bahorik

Claudia J. Bahorik is a retired family physician who traded her stethoscope in for a pen a few years ago. Dr. Bahorik is actually working on a B.A. in Professional Writing at Penn State Berks and still trying to find an agent for her two unpublished manuscripts.

"Trump" art by Naomi Vogels

Trickster, Liar, Thief

Trickster, liar, thief
Rants and raves as if
He possesses the Truth
Fake News rolls out of
His mouth abundantly,
Incessantly, until there is
No line between, rhyme, or
Reason for what he says
Spontaneously, in Tweets,
And arrogant Words,
He speaks with forked tongue
Walking on the hot coals of
HELL
Submitting to the devil,
The evil that can lurk and
Take control in men's hearts
A paradox, a battle for
Life and will
Like a typical Gemini torn
Between his two selves
A great teacher for
Humanity and All Being
Uniting us in God
To save ourselves from
Sabotage and self-destruction

~ © 2018 Michael Barnett

Rev. Michael Barnett has written poetry since a child. As an instrument of Spirit, he watches and observes what is occurring in the world and how we can effectively bring about loving and healing change. He works for social justice, women's rights, and creating the sacred marriage within.

"Ya Drivin' Me Crazy!" art by Barrie Maguire

Challenges, Tempests, and Petty Annoyances   21

POST-TRUTH DISCOURSE

2016 entry, Oxford English Dictionary: objective facts less influential in sharing public opinion than appeals to emotion

"It's-huge-it's-gonna-be-great,"
no one asks about the "it."
So the huge-it's-gonna-be-great
gets dragged through the gate,
the Greeks pour out and flash goes Troy.
Hags in the woods screech
"It's-huge-it's-gonna-be-great,"
promise, cajole, beseech.
Baptized by bombast and blood lust,
the Thane of Cawdor converts
and summarily snuffs out a dynasty.
The "it" joined at the hip
with the vaguest of verbs
spumes and spews false claims,
lethal adjectives, and
the "huge-it's-gonna-be-great" con triumphs
in the Post-truth swamp, and the O.E.D.

~ *Virginia Beards*

Virginia draws from an archive of urban (New York, Philadelphia), suburban (Seattle), rural (Lancaster county, PA), and international experience (Denmark, France, North Africa) plus a considerable literary backlog acquired as a member of the Penn State English Department for twenty-three years. She has published criticism in <u>The Journal of Modern Literature</u>, <u>Twentieth Century Views of Women Writers</u>, and in <u>Critique: Studies in Modern Fiction.</u> Her poetry has appeared in <u>Writing on the Edge </u>(Univ. of California, Davis and in <u>Provoke, #3,</u> the journal of <u>Backlash Press)</u>; her short stories in <u>Chester County Fiction</u>. She holds a M.A. from the University of Pennsylvania and a Ph.D. from Bryn Mawr College.

Digital Art "Almighty" by Sue DaNym

The Big Hype

It was the stock in trade of politicians and always had been. It had become the stock in trade of Corporate America, which guides the making of the nation's laws and the formulation of its policies more surely than any number or combination of voters and elected officials. And it had become the stock in trade of most of its citizens, especially the young. We are no longer judged by our actions; we are judged by our image—or so we hope. We don't invade and occupy other nations if we say that we're keeping the rest of the world safe from terrorists with weapons of mass destruction. We don't exploit sweatshop labor in Third-World countries if we say that we're practicing free-market principles, promoting the marvels of globalization, and increasing the wealth of our shareholders. We don't have the largest income gap, the poorest bottom fifth of the population, or the largest proportion of citizens without adequate medical insurance of any Western nation if we invoke the bogeyman of socialism in order to preserve the status quo. We are who and what we say we are. What we actually do is irrelevant.

If, for example, you were looking to move up into a higher socio-economic class, Robertson* knew that you would have a lot more ground to cover in the U.S. than in Europe. We have the greatest disparity between rich and poor of any industrialized Western democracy. Nearly a fifth of Americans live in poverty, a higher rate than that of any other modern Western nation.[2] And there is actually greater socio-economic mobility in Europe than in the United States, especially from one generation to the next.[3]

Unlike the vast majority of industrialized nations, the U.S. not only has no laws mandating paid holidays, sick days, or vacations for workers, but also no laws providing for paid maternity leave from one's job, much less paternity leave. Working people in the Land of Family Values would undoubtedly be surprised, one author noted, if they had any idea of the accommodations employers make for parenthood on the other side of the Atlantic.[4]

There are more physicians per hundred thousand people in Europe than in the United States; and historically, the U.S. has been the only modern, industrialized democracy besides South Africa that did not guarantee all its citizens equal access to health care.[5] Life expectancy for both sexes is greater in Europe than in the United States.[6] Infant mortality, he had read for years, is lower virtually everywhere in Western Europe than it is here. And so-on.

We are number one, however, in such categories as billions spent on the nation's military budget, pounds of garbage produced per person on an annual basis, the divorce rate, and the pregnancy rate among teen-agers.[7] Furthermore, the rate of homicide in the U.S. is about four times what it is among the countries of the European Union.[8] And the U.S. is way out in front of everyone else in both the number and percentage of its citizens who are behind bars. Even China trailed by a considerable margin.[9] Predictably enough, we also have more lawyers for every thousand citizens than any country in the industrialized world.[10]

Yes indeed, Robertson thought. Keep convincing yourself, America. Keep repeating the chant over and over: "We're Number One! We're Number one!" Secure in your isolation, your news media largely ignoring events and conditions in the rest of the world, you'll never know any better. Your politicians will reassure you. Corporate America will reassure you. Television, radio, and the print media will reassure you. And most likely your friends, your neighbors, and your family will reassure you as well. But on what basis, he had to wonder. By what standard of measurement? According to what system of values?

--adapted from the book Nights on the Mountain, a spiritual journey by Craig H. Bennett

*Hal Robertson is the narrative voice/center of consciousness in Nights on the Mountain.

[2]*Hutton, Will. A Declaration of Interdependence. New York: W.W. Norton, 2003 p.130*

[3]*Hill, Steven. Europe's Promise. Berkeley: University of California, 2010 p.100*

[4] Rifkin, Jeremy. *The European Dream.* New York: Tarcher/Penguin, 2004 p.43; Hill, *Promise* p. 73. Further corroboration of much of the comparative data between the U.S. and countries of the EU included in this chapter can be found in Wilkinson, Richard and Kate Pickett. *The Spirit Level*. New York: Bloomsbury Press, 2009.

[5] Rifkin, *Dream* p.80

[6] Rifkin, *Dream* p.79; Hill, *Promise* p.137

[7] "Snapshot" *U.S. News*; Stobbe, Mike (AP). "4 in 10 babies in U.S. born to unwed mothers."The Philadelphia *Inquirer* 22 Nov. 2006 A8

[8] Rifkin, *Dream* p.81

[9] Aizenman, N.C. (*Washington Post*). "Record inmate count in U.S." The Philadelphia *Inquirer* 29 Feb 2008 A1

[10] "Snapshot" *U.S. News*; Hutton, *Declaration* p.141

~ Craig H. Bennett

Craig H. Bennett, author of Nights on the Mountain, a spiritual journey *holds degrees from Ursinus and Johns Hopkins. He has a substantial background in music, has worked as a professional on-camera and voice-over performer in Philadelphia and New York, and is retired from the faculty of Valley Forge Military College. He has traveled extensively in Europe, visited the former Soviet Union, and participated in an expedition to the dry tropical wilderness of northeastern Brazil on the trail of Col. Percival H. Fawcett, who disappeared in 1925 while searching for the lost city he designated as "Z."*

"Words Hurt" art by Katie Hamburger

The Evening News

It simmers silently, my seething rage.
Roiling.
Boiling.

Offenses bubbling through my consciousness-- the racist
 assumptions and misogynistic dismissals seeped from
 self-serving lip; sealed indictments against them.

Rumbling defenses stumble over themselves, scrumming to
 respond...but facts don't matter and the truth is fake news.

The surreal unconscionability swirls inside my headspace--a
centrifugal force--steam screams mercilessly: this vessel a siren.

Listeners struck still
In sonic shock until...
Silence.

And when society re-centers civility,
 set as sacrosanct the remembrance that Revolution starts as a
  silently simmering rage.

~ *Jessica Bergeman*

Jessica is a proud graduate of the Boyertown School District, where she first found joy in written expression and public speaking through the Optimist Oratorical Program. She built upon her BASH education at Vassar College with degrees in Political Science, Africana Studies, and Women's Studies, and finalized it at the Beasley School of Law at Temple University, after which she prosecuted criminals as an Assistant State's Attorney in Chicago. (Pro tip: jury trials are a wonderful opportunity to perfect those Oratorical skills!) Jess currently practices Mediation and Regulatory Compliance law for the State of Texas, enjoys the live music scene in Austin, and refuses to leave the warm weather--much to her mother's chagrin.

"Year of the Dog" art by Kathi Ember

*Full color prints are available
by emailing politikatart@gmail.com.
Or on Instagram as politikatart.*

"You're Fired"

We are tired and poor,
humbled and sick,
huddling in masses
because you are thick.

With alternative facts
you stole the election
as we gathered in streets
for peace and connection.

An attack by your people
killed one of our kind.
You are an infection
of a hateful mind.

You cooked the books,
with Putin you fiddle.
Scum rises to the top
like fat on the griddle.

You don't know the job
and think you are king,
undoing what good men
put together again.

You've got no respect;
just grab what you need,
even if we reject

your unwanted seed.

You're rude, a bully,
with the culture of a thug.
You are not fitting.
We must pull the plug.

So stand in the street,
take that shot.
You've already murdered
our youngest lot.

But most of all
I will never forgive,
how you revived a HATE
that should never live.

Photoshopped pictures to prove
followers confused
Hypnotized by "Faux News"
Your ego is bruised

Last time we were proud,
happy for the Black Man.
The world cheered out loud!
He said "Yes We Can!"

You'll go down in history
the most hated man.
We thought it was Hitler,
but your hands are littler.

People surround you,
their patience is tired.
Me Too! Time's up!
Ha, You're Fired!

~ *Susan Biebuyck*

Together in 2008 Susan & Jane founded Studio B in which is a non-profit, community-run gallery located in the heart of historic Boyertown, Pennsylvania. The gallery supports a healthy and thriving artists' membership. Susan has curated more than 100 exhibits to uphold Studio B's mission which is to promote art and artists from the local area.

This is the 5th Art Responding to Literature and Literature Responding to Art that Susan and Jane have put together.

"Granny Smith" art by Susan Biebuyck

Dear Mr. Smith

I can't understand
How a man
Can earn his Honor
With his hands
When ours is believed
To be between our legs

Men receive praise
We receive scorn

Double standard rolls off
The tongue
Much too easily

Even my teacher
Once told me
"Oh! No, you don't get to do that!
It's much too unbecoming
Of a lady."

What is?
Fucking missionary?

I'm sure that's how you see it Mr. L

Try comparing me to a chewed-up apple now

~ Aubrey I. Butto

Aubrey I. Butto is a Berks County native. She is presently studying Modern Languages and Cultures and English at The Virginia Military Institute. She writes poetry in her free time and in her Poetry and Ways of Reading classes.

Poster from the march, "Pussy" art by Mary Salen

#NotYouToo

Did I smile too brightly?

Hold eye contact too long?

Did I walk across the room,

Through the hall,

Down the street

A little too seductively?

Was my sweater too tight?

My skirt too short?

What made you think I was interested?

In your compliments

In your leering looks

In your grabby hands

In you, like that?

I trusted you

Respected you as a colleague

Liked you for a friend

Loved you like a father

Slut, tease, stuck up whore

I must have done something

To earn those names

The unwanted attention

From friends

From strangers

From family

So I dimmed my smile

Used it cautiously

I built up walls

So you couldn't see

The real me

The bright,

shiny,

passionate me

#Time's Up

The walls are tumbling down

The light is shining through

If that's a problem

It's not me

It's *you*

~ ***Patty Kline-Capaldo***

Patty Kline-Capaldo is a writer, teacher, and creativity coach. Her passion is supporting writers and visual artists in their creative endeavors. Patty hosts two Meetup groups, where writers and artists gather for instruction, mutual encouragement, and inspiration: Just Write (http://www.meetup.com/Just-Write-in-Collegeville-PA) and The Artist's Way Circle (http://www.meetup.com/The-Artists-Way-Circle-in-Collegeville-PA/). She has also taught writing classes at Chester County Night School. Two of her memoir pieces have been published in anthologies: "Legacy of a Childless Woman" in <u>Slants of Light, Stories and Poems From the Women's Writing Circle</u> and "My Father's Daughter" in <u>The Life Unexpected, A Collection of Stories and Poems</u>. Patty earned her BA degree in Journalism and History from Indiana University and teacher certification from Ursinus College. She lives in Pottstown, PA, with her husband, Rich, and their three cats—Sarah, Splash, and Snapple. Read Patty's blog at http://pattyklinecapaldo.com/blog/.

"Above a Single Day" **art by Adriano Farinella**

Cloud Seeding

Do not step on my dream.
You need not understand it.
You need not agree with it.
All you need to do is let it breathe.

Do not step on my dream.
I may change my mind.
I may be a complete failure.
Or I may succeed gloriously.

Do not step on my dream.
It comes from a place deep inside.
It is fragile and terrified of the light.
It needs nurturing and support to grow.

Do not step on my dream.
I will keep it close to me.
I will hide it from the world.
I will believe when no one else can.

Do not step on my dream.
It sustains me.
It enriches me.
It makes me your friend.

~ Patricia D'Innocenzo

"Chicken Head" art by Angela Faust-Izzo

What's for Dinner?

I am tired of chicken.

I am tired of looking at it. I am tired of eating it. I am tired of hearing how good it is for me – minus the crispy skin of course. I am tired of it at banquets. I am tired of nuggets and sandwiches and pizza and wraps. I am tired of chicken gussied up for dinner and the remains in salad for lunch. I am tired of a whole chicken for Sunday dinner.

I don't care if it is versatile. I don't care if you can prepare it 5,000 ways. I don't care if you can get it "buy one, get one free." I don't care if everyone eats it. I don't care if you can eat it hot or cold.

Admit it. You look at those pale, limp, boneless chicken breasts and say "What do I do with them this time?" You look at a menu – 5 out of 7 salads have chicken, 4 out of 6 sandwiches have chicken. They haven't figured out how to make it into dessert but give them time.

It is lunch food, picnic food, dinner food, portable food, fancy food, wedding food and sick food as chicken soup.

They say computers are going to take over. They are wrong. It is chicken.

~ *Patricia D'Innocenzo*

Patricia D'Innocenzo is the author of poems and non-fiction that have been published in several anthologies including <u>Snowflakes and Ribbons</u> and <u>Autumn Magic</u>. She is currently working on her first novel and a book of her poems accompanied by her own photographs. She has lived in the Phoenixville area for over twenty years.

"Stick a Pin in IT!" & "The Ephing SLF"
art by Susan Biebuyck

SPOTTED LANTERNFLY

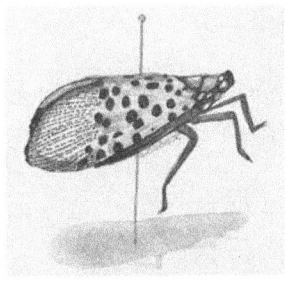

When I first heard of you, Lycorma delicatula, with your orange wings, your little legs, I thought it impossible that you could rise to power, that you could take over our land, destroy what good had grown, leaving your oozing piles of excretions on our once beautiful world.

You're a shape shifter, progressing through instar stages as the season heats up until without paying any price, you've escaped what you were and become larger, more destructive. You've grown wings, and with them, the increased ability to escape paying the price for what you've done. In your slow, dawdling flight—somehow—you escape capture, evade consequence for the destruction you've wrought. You have an army of others just like you to replace the few that have been squashed.

In my quest to fight for our trees, our fruit—to restore our land to what it was— I attend meetings, scrape your eggs from trunks of host trees, cut down tree-of-heaven to limit your power. Yet you push on, reaching farther, the quarantine zone expanding. You create war zones where there were none. You breed, send your minions to do your work, wreak havoc, spread wrath.

But you, spotted lanternfly, have given one beautiful gift.

In this season of hate and idiocy, this time when common sense and kindness, justice and equality have been replaced by tweets and bullying, roll backs of rights and regulations, you have given us the gift of something to squash, to smash, something to do when the world feels entirely broken, some action to take when all we try to teach our children fails.

We smash, crush, squish—with shoes, books, bare hands— in the name of making the world a better place.

You let us rant—let us rage.

~ *Heather Goodman*

Heather E. Goodman's fiction is forthcoming or has been published in <u>Witness</u>, <u>Gray's Sporting Journal</u>, <u>Shenandoah</u>, <u>Hunger Mountain</u>, <u>Crab Orchard Review</u>, and the <u>Chicago Tribune</u>, where her story won the Nelson Algren Award. She teaches creative writing, tutors, and lives along the Manatawny Creek with her husband Paul and pooch Leo. Please visit: www.heatheregoodman.com.

Lemon Twist

The doorman stood at the entrance letting the residents walk through while life and love played games with their hearts. He tipped his hat to each person hiding the twinkle in his eye. Holding the door open a little farther than normal allowed the breeze to disrupt the typical arrangement of meeting notices and ads on the bulletin board. One yellow flyer waved at Marcia when she left the elevator. She clutched her satchel with one hand while buttoning her blazer with the other. Her mother's words from last night's call still stung. *Your biological clock is ticking. Focusing on your career won't bring me a grandbaby.* Her calls didn't always include this reminder, but at least once a week she would slip in the ticking sound amidst her gossip from the neighborhood. Tick tock tick tock.

Maybe the yellow color drew Marcia close, but the words sucked her in all the way. Lemon Twist. Turn your sweet tart into a sweet heart. Come let Lemon show you how she found love. Marcia's finger traced the hearts decorating the bottom of the page when a woman decked out in jogging clothes approached.

"That's a good group. That's where I met my husband," she said. "It's just down the road."

"What does the group do?" Marcia asked. The words slipped out before she could stop herself.

"They give you advice on how to attract your soul-mate; they tell you what worked for them. Gotta run!"

She dashed out the door before Marcia could ask more. Advice tossed out to her from strangers usually didn't stick. Her defenses had grown so thick that uninvited words bounced off her. This time, they touched a soft spot in her chest and she decided to swing by after work.

"A Life Full of Color" art by Heather Lippincott Foust

*

    Later that day, Marcia stood in the gymnasium down the block from her apartment building watching the people mingle. She held her black coat draped over her arm in front of her as a shield. The weight of it reminded her of the loneliness and frustration heaped on her back. Her dreams of finding love had somehow not come to fruition and she hoped this group would show her how to send positive vibes out into the universe. This idea, that you could send some kind of invisible message to attract someone, would work or so she had heard.

The crowd around her didn't exactly come off as polished and successful. One woman wore sandals with white socks and cargo pants with tissues and crayons sticking out of the pockets. The yellow peace sign on her t-shirt looked faded from excessive washing. After glancing up at Marcia, she stepped over to introduce herself.

"Hi, I'm Lemon! Welcome! Are you looking for love?" She reached her hand out to Marcia. Her nails were painted bright yellow.

"Umm, yes." Marcia shook her hand and felt a shiver go up her back.

"Great. This is the place for you! What's your name?" Lemon motioned for Marcia to move toward the circle of chairs.

"Marcia Cooper." She moved forward but her feet stuck to the floor as if she walked through molasses.

"Nice to meet you." Lemon turned to arrange the chairs and kept mumbling to herself. "I'm Lemon. My name is Lemon. This is the place for you. Hello, I'm Lemon."

The stale air, spiked with an occasional whiff of cologne, kept Marcia searching for a fan to turn on. Footsteps echoed across the room amplifying the hollow feeling in Marcia's heart.

"Those of you new here, come sit on the chairs," Lemon said. "The others stand outside the group and be ready to speak."

The group parted with some people sitting on the creaking metal chairs and others shuffling to their spots behind. The ones sitting stared at each other trying to understand what was happening. Lemon turned her attention back to Marcia.

"You come stand here in the middle."

What have I gotten myself into, Marcia thought.

Being surrounded by strangers made her feel claustrophobic despite the large space. Convinced that the piercing eyes could see her every mistake and flaw, she avoided eye contact and instead focused on the dead moth lying on the floor outside the circle.

Lemon whistled to get everyone's attention. "We'll go around in a circle and one by one give Marcia the advice that helped us find our loving partner. If you have something specific that will help her, speak up! We'll continue to go around until the timer rings. Let's begin."

The people on the outskirts of the circle shouted advice.

"Be more vocal," a woman said in a voice so soft Marcia could barely hear.

"Try new things," said one man whose stomach oozed over his belt. He wore a shirt so tight the buttons threatened to pop and fling into someone's eye.

"Go to bars." The man who said this held a small flask in his hand and took a drink after he spoke.

"Be a little taller." This came from a woman with platform shoes and a denim jumpsuit, the opposite of Marcia's style.

"Fix your hair," a woman said, who had stringy uncombed hair and streaks of makeup down her cheeks.

One woman who twisted a long strand of hair around her finger said in a sultry voice, "Tell a white lie."

These absurd comments itched at Marcia's skin. She rubbed her arms to brush them off. She squeezed her eyes shut and tried to imagine herself somewhere else–anywhere else. The timer had to go off any second, didn't it? She didn't know how much more of this she could take.

"Drop your books on a man's foot."

"Wear more makeup."

Marcia held her breath. Her pulse raced and she felt herself shrinking in her spot. Her hands reached out to balance herself as her head spun.

"Dress up every day."

"Lower your standards."

"Accept any attention you get."

Marcia forced herself to take a deep breath and regain her composure. Suddenly, an image of her grandmother popped into her head and Marcia heard her wise words blocking out all the others. *Be yourself! It's better to be alone than to be with someone you don't like! Love yourself first!*

The thought of her grandmother made Marcia smile. She could almost smell her cherry blossom dusting powder. She straightened herself and snickered before facing them with her rebuttal.

"No, you're all wrong. You don't know what you're talking about. I'm not changing. I need to find someone that loves me just as I am. I know who I am. I am smart. I am strong. I am powerful. I am love. I am beautiful. I am authentic!"

Marcia grinned at the shocked looks on their faces. Annoyance bubbled up from her and she dropped it all on them. It was not a burden she intended to take with her. She left them brewing and broke through the circle. When she reached the door, she pulled on her coat and took another deep breath before she turned and yelled, "You better add some sugar; your group is too sour."

She stepped out onto the sidewalk and exhaled. She turned and walked toward her apartment building. Only a few steps from the door, a gush of wind caught her breath so she turned around and held her hair out of her eyes. When the wind calmed down, she spun back and bumped into a man bundled up in a black coat and scarf.

"Pardon me," he said.

"Excuse me. Sorry," Marcia said. She moved back onto an uneven part of the sidewalk and almost tumbled.

The man reached out and held her elbow to help her balance. "You look distraught. Don't tell me. You were in the Lemon Twist meeting, weren't you?"

"Yes, I was. How do you know about that?" Marcia asked. She pulled her coat tighter around her. She looked down at her shoes and stepped farther away from him.

"My roommate roped me into going one time. He thought I needed help meeting someone." He raised his hands up and stepped back. "I hated it."

"I did too," Marcia said. She glanced up at his angled features, lightly covered with stubble.

He shook his head. "I hate people giving advice like that. Mind your own business is what I told them."

"I've always thought meeting someone should happen naturally, don't you agree?" Marcia asked.

He reached up and rubbed his chin. "I agree. Absolutely." He reached out his hand to Marcia. "I'm Andrew. Andrew Chase."

Marcia accepted his handshake and when their hands connected, for a moment, nothing else existed in the world. Maybe the world was sweet after all. After turning back toward her apartment, the two of them stood side by side when the doorman caught her eye. He tipped his hat to her and winked.

~Sharon Hajj

Sharon Hajj is the author of <u>The Clock Tower</u>, a middle-grade fantasy. Her short story, "The Time Keeper" appears in <u>Freshly Brewed Fiction Volume #1</u>. Both of these are available at Towne Book Center & Café in Collegeville. Sharon writes mostly for children but ventures into other genres in her short stories, some of which are available in online publications. She enjoys writing, daydreaming, hiking, and spending time with her family. Her pets are quite fun as long as the cats are not walking across the computer keyboard. She is a member of Just Write writing group and the Women's National Book Association - Greater Philadelphia Chapter. For more about this author, visit her website at www.sharonhajj.com.

"Be Free" art by Marta Herman

POEMS 1 AND 2

1.
The life of man
Is no more
No less

But every bit
As powerful

As a blade
of grass -

2.
Beware the danger
Of the innocents
For the gentle curve
Of a sea shell
Will steal your gaze
And break our heart
To pieces –

*~ **Marta Herman***

Marta started writing poems after a totally life-changing month, experiencing the powerful nature of Southern Africa . . . powerful and pure, loving and cruel, always filled with infinite mysteries. Upon returning, she developed a process of watercolor painting that helps to bring forth visions and thoughts from heart and mind. These, which she calls "Mind Pictures" are accompanied by humorous poems.

"Sugar Jacket" art by Susan Biebuyck

IWONTPUTONMYSUGARJACKETDOTCOM

in the vein of sofia vergara while
she plays gloria pritchett, i won't

put on my sugar jacket. that kind
of medicine doesn't really work

for long, it turns out. my newest goal
is to squeeze my eyelids shut hard

in hopes that you'll
burst into beautiful

iridescent bubbles,
if you are in fact

mind-numbing
as a curse word.

that's me turning
a negative into

a positive if i can't
get rid of your tedium.

~ jennifer hetrick

RANT POEM NO. 17

once you find someone certifiably
annoying, how do you come back
from that—i don't know. when you
have an overly orange and far from
not-crazy person leading your country,

how do you come back from that,
too—i'm still waiting for this answer,
the change needed and how it would
roll out. i can't imagine it yet. but it's
critical. i'm sure i'm not alone in that

thought-boat. and why use a turn signal
—it isn't a universal symbol to let others
know what you're doing on the road so
they can make sure to not hit your car
or be smashed into by yours or anything

like that. but maybe to survive, i'll dive
into a positive rant, if there is such a thing.
i'll thank the sun for the brief seconds i
can spend time with it in the morning
before i go sit in a building all day. i love

your light, i'll tell it. to the sky, know that
you keep me grounded. and the same to
the grass when i rest my spine against its
blades. comedy, you save me, too. and
laughter is the smoothest pill, the one i

take to not overdose eye-wise and into
the collective mental illness stirred by
the one now supposedly in charge, who
used to like, way too much, any chance

to say to people that they were fired.

in the words of a bumper sticker taped
to a sedan parked next to my sidewalk,
just be nice. (or leave.) (really, though.)

~ *jennifer hetrick*

Jennifer Hetrick believes in promoting what's useful across the invisible lines following language's ties between people. Through grants from the Pennsylvania Council on the Arts and Berks Arts Council, Jennifer recently completed a three-year project called <u>the labors of our fingertips: poems from manufacturing history in berks county</u>. As a visiting artist taking poetry into schools and state parks, she also teaches a traveling poetry class in wandering efforts around the region.

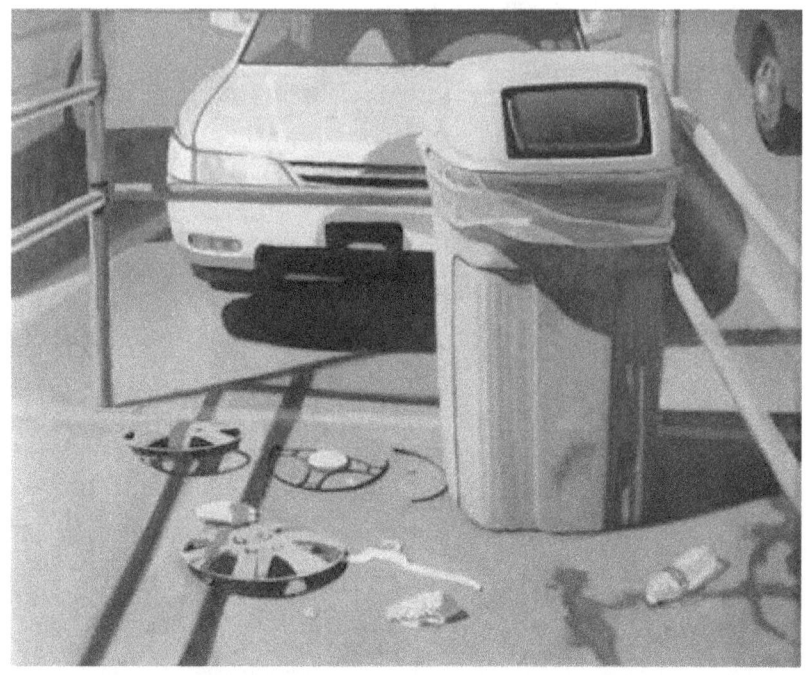

"Come On, People!" art by Daniel Gorman

Challenges, Tempests, and Petty Annoyances

You Say, Rant! Rant!

The email asks to put my peeves in prose
I think for some time and then, I suppose
I'll try. I'll try.
And I do. I give it shot. Knowing full well, a poet I am not.
I try to please Jane, so I vent and complain.
You say, Rant! Rant!
I say, I Can't! Can't!

My youthful angst has eased so well
I simply never tell others to "got to hell."
I am more gentle now…and much more kind
Age has removed me from the grind.
You say, Rant! Rant!
I say, I Can't! Can't!

Do things not drive me crazy?
Or am I just too lazy?
I'll try. I'll try.

Robocalls that never stop
Deer consuming all my crop
Shopping carts that dent my car
A thousand TVs in my bar
Newspaper articles long as a book
Parents never stopping to cook

Inept people in positions of power
A five-minute call that takes an hour
Uncurbed dogs that poop and poop
Unleashed dogs that travel in a group
Drive thru windows with long, long lines
Loving neighbors who don't pull their blinds
Express lane shoppers with topped off carts
Discourteous people who have no hearts
The baseball game with changing rules
DIY projects without the tools
You say, Rant! Rant!
I say, I Can't! Can't!

But when a parent ignores a child who is raging
And a child ignores a parent who is aging
I can text, that I am vexed.
Add racism, ageism, sexism to this note
And I confess that gets my goat.
Another thing that makes me bitter
Is people who choose to litter
Even more so…people who don't control their twitter.
I tried to Rant! I tried to Rant!
I cannot say I Can't. I Can't.

~ *Annarose Ingarra-Milch*

Annarose Ingarra-Milch is a nationally-recognized inspirational speaker and the author of the award-winning novel "Lunch with Lucille." She is a retired law enforcement officer, serial entrepreneur, positive aging advocate, webcaster, TEDx presenter, state pageant queen, community volunteer, coach, wife, mother, and now poetess. 'You say, Rant! Rant!' is Annarose's first adventure into poetry. "Although I think of myself more as a storyteller than a poet, I am reminded of what the poet, writer, educator Sarah Kay says about what storytellers and poets have in common, 'They had something to say, and did.'"

BE FEARLESS

We humans are a funny lot

If you see fear in animals

It's fear of us

If you see fear in humans

It's because of us

Fear of each other

Inhibits us

Limits what we can

Achieve

Climb a mountain

See the view from above

The rising of the sun

The setting

The moon that gives us light

In the darkest of nights

Embrace it all

Delve into the depths

Of possibilities

Of

No fear

~ L. T. James

"Blanca" art by Sue Ciccone

L.T. James has traveled around the world mostly on her own by sea, land, air, and on foot working, writing, photographing, and getting to know people of all different cultures and beliefs. Her work as Command Liaison for the Navy and Marine Corps led her to Japan for a three-year tour of duty where she also taught English and stayed in a monastery high in the "Himalayas" of Japan. She returned to her hometown of Reading because of her deep roots, the generous and welcoming people, and the amazingly beautiful landscapes. She now leads the Pagoda Writers group each month and writes poetry when inspiration comes.

"TechVanitas-Gray Typewriter" *photograph by Jeanette May*

Challenges, Tempests, and Petty Annoyances

To the Man on the Phone at the Pennsylvania Cultural Data Base who said, "How may I help you," and "Have a nice day," While I Worked on Submitting a Grant.

I know you feel out of control.
I can tell by the way you've
Defined your job, your life, as
Responding to questions
About a computer program.

What I really wanted,
What you really wanted,
Was to not be having a conversation.

Your program had decided I hadn't
Stroked a key in twenty minutes.
It logged me out of a session.
I called you up and you logged me
Back into the computer.

We both wanted to do something
Meaningful with our lives,
But you must be beyond that now,
Content to feel purposeful
Restoring my computer session
And pretending to be cheerful.

When are engineers and programmers
Going to quit messing with our lives?

We've all met them, haven't we?
I have two in my family now...
They visit, but they're not very good at
Human relationships;
Not very good at... what's the word?

Oh, yes, affection. They're not good at
Interpersonal tenderness.

And it's getting overwhelming, isn't it?
Trying to understand the changes
Computer programmers and
Computer engineers have imposed.

I wanted a simpler life.
But instead of meeting my needs
By pulling the plug at your end of the machine,
You plugged me back in,
Returning me to Dante's Ninth Level of Hell,
The one reserved for Traitors.
Which, instead of brimming with ice,
Is a computer maze I was completing
In order to apply for a grant.

You did exactly as I requested,
But I wanted more from you.

I can't stop this from my end.
I have kids, a mortgage, things to buy.
And if I tried…
If I even thought of trying…
I'd have to take a step
I can't quite take.

I tell myself that these changes
Are just the Universe Blossoming,
As if picturing flowers solves the problem
Of spinning out of control.

No, I want you to Save me
Because I don't think I can save myself.

I can't get off of the roller coaster.
It's moving too fast.
This computer world
Gives the illusion
That we're going somewhere
As if there is a somewhere to get to
That isn't located between our ears.

Why didn't you
Read between the lines
When I called?
Don't you see that all of us
Need to take two steps backwards?

Please, I beg you,
Step away from your computer.
Ask your manager to back
Out of our lives.
Please, grant this favor
Before all warmth
In human contact
Drains out
Through the heat-sink
That is technology.

~ *Marilyn L.T. Klimcho*

Marilyn L.T. Klimcho is the Treasurer of Berks Bards, Inc., a grassroots poetry group centered in Reading. In addition to writing poetry, she also writes short stories and has recently tackled writing a screenplay. Her work in short story was nominated for a Pushcart Prize by the <u>Schuylkill Valley Journal</u>.

POLITICIANS

"Biting Mad!" art by Jim Meehan

Politicians are a sorry lot.
They preach, promise, and predict
they're here to serve us
but they act like rock stars.
They feel privileged,
live better than we do, and live longer.
Running for re-election, they're boring
promising everything, giving us mostly nothing but excuses.
Give me something -
A train conductor yelling "all aboard"
A squeaky violin
A kid scratching his fingers over a slate blackboard
An umpire yelling "You're Out"
A race horse's fart in his stall
An auctioneer begging for a bid.
Give me anything,
Anything but these guys.

~ Ollie Koehler

REINCARNATION

The idea seemed appealing
But not for me.
Wait a minute
What if I came back
To meet all my worldly nightmares
And none of the joys.
That crabby eighth grade teacher - she's back.
The town bully down the lane
There's that know-it-all wind bag
Pontificating for hours saying nothing
There she is going down the street
That nosey gossiping neighbor lady
In her white anklets and baggy flowered wash dress
Still telling lies and creating chaos
The misery of air travel
Packed into a long aluminum tube like a
    can of King Oscar Sardines
Being put on hold - Press 5, Press 6, Press 7
Filing another income tax return
No, I'm staying here
I've been there, done that.

~ Ollie Koehler

The late Harold "Ollie" Koehler began his writing career at age 78 and became a prize-winning poet. In 2015, he won first prize in the Berks Encore Senior Poetry Contest and shared third place in 2016. His poetry has appeared in <u>Muse: The Inspirations of Our Lives</u>, published in 2017 by Studio B Fine Art Gallery. Ollie was the owner of Ollie's Barber Stylist and owned several other businesses. He enjoyed many art-related hobbies, visiting art exhibits and museums, traveling, and attending the Metropolitan Opera and Opera Philadelphia. Ollie passed away at 81 on January 31, 2018.

Anticipating that he may not live to see his current poems in this volume, Ollie ordered and paid for copies of <u>Let's Rant! Challenges, Tempests and Petty Annoyances</u> to be sent to his family. Rest in peace, Ollie. You will remain alive and well in our memories. ~ Jane

"Butterflies Journey of Love" art by Jillian Wright-Prout

Come On Now

If I was still alive
I'd give everything I've got
To find out what it's like
To be ages ahead of my time
So far ahead in fact that
No one I'd know would like me
I'd love to be that out of step

Right this moment
I'm not so sure that people
Are the only living things that add up by subtracting
Because I've seen snails cross each other's
Slime
And ferns that wilt all together
It must be strange
To live your life
For what will never happen

To be honest
What I'd do if I could is this -
Die again for much much more
Be thunder from the inside
Or go so far beyond all that
That echoes couldn't find me.

~ Hiram Larew

"Berks View" art by Lynn Millar

SILLY

Look here
You love him like the farm and candy
And he is crazy about you alright
Everyone knows it out loud already
Except you two mudbirds

And of course far be it for me to suggest that you perk
    up in time
But goodness come on -
The ducks are about to waddle away
Ghosts are chuckling behind you
And even your good great Aunt Polly
Is twiddling her strings

You know how everyone says life is too short for this
    and that
Well for once they're more right than wrong -
So is it really going to take me dragging you ears first
To that door
To do what's needed
Because dear sweet chicken of all
It's nearly eight oh my thirty.

~ Hiram Larew

Larew's work has appeared most recently in Honest Ulsterman, Amsterdam Quarterly, FORTH, Viator *and* Two Hawks Quarterly. *He lives in Maryland and is a global food security specialist.*

"Winter's Incipience" art by Tamie Dickson

ROUGE

I am in a fetal position, encased in an icy sheath. Spring no longer is within my frigid grasp. Crimson cascades down the tips of my rigid fingers.

Will mother ever return from her December slumber; will she come back and embrace me, melting this winter that has settled into my bones.

They say I am unique, but I know this agony must torment others. The canvas, I painted, with the Jackson Pollock flailing of exposed arteries has been on exhibit for hours, and my critics have cringed at its morbidity.

My muse has withered, beneath the dead leaves of homicidal Autumn.

I implore you to return with sutures and sunbeams. I am bent. I am broken. I am still. I am breathless. A tardy April has stolen the fog from my lungs.

("Rouge" is an ekphrastic poem inspired by a photograph by Tamie Dickson entitled "Winter's Incipience.")

~ Catherine Mahony

Catherine Mahony, a writer in multiple genres, is finishing a bachelor's degree in professional writing at Kutztown University. She holds Associate in Arts degrees in Communications and Liberal Arts from Reading Area Community College, where she received the Creative Writing Award for academic excellence in both 2013 and 2014. Mahony earned two awards from the Community College Humanities Association for pieces that appeared in Legacy, *RACC's literary journal, and was a finalist in the 2014 Norman Mailer High School and College Awards Competition in the category of Creative Nonfiction. She has also been published in* Front Street Journal, Nota Bene, Agony and Ecstasy: Reflections Inspired by Our Lives, Layers of Language: Idioms and Favorite Expressions, To Be: Know Thyself, You Do You, Muse: The Inspirations of Our Lives *and* Lehigh Valley Vanguard. *Cat's first chapbook of poetry entitled "Prior Restraints," contains compelling images taken by local photographer, Tamie Dickson. Mahony has shared her writing, which depicts her struggles with addiction and mental illness, with women incarcerated within the Berks County Jail System.*

"Sofie on the Wall" art by Matt Smith

Fall Poem

Do you feel that is how they found each other?

        with an air of hope,

                Yes, I feel they both shared a need for a healthy home.

        Bare on his
        bed sheets,

he pauses to ask
permission to enter

                my body.

                I am immediately
                overcome with
                the need

for him

                to be within
                the walls
                of me.

        We collide
        gracefully

as he raises

                me, I am numb

        through the motions
        of constrained relief.
        Exasperatedly,

Baby, what is it that I have to do to get you to cum?

            Taken aback at the realization
            of having been genuinely seen,
            I like you, with a contradicting
            smile. By the window, I stood,
        walls rising
where they had only slightly
        begun to fall

                and I feel

his eyes

                on my spine
                and I watch

        the city, the sky,
        the stars behind darkness
        an attempt to pull them out
        with pure will—
        interrupted,

*Come back to bed,
you are too sexy
to be all the way
by the window.*

                Another smile,
                as it is sometimes nice
                to be bodies with bodies,
                I return

        bare on his bed sheets,
        skin soft lips heated thighs
        wrapped in sleep.

I haven't seen you in weeks,
he says,
                                        though I could say the same,
                                                          so I do.
                        The need to disappear, as apparitions
                             to one another and the world. He avoids
                             hovering over the disappointment of shared
                          silence and moves to the normal human notion of:
How have you been?
                                              Filterless asymmetry, eyes
                                              falling toward the floor:
                                                          I'm okay.
                        With a shift in the air,
What, what is it?
                              Waiting in line
                              is not the place
                              and in any case,
he knows
                        I do not have the words.
                                              Though, eyes naturally
                                              ricochet off the floor
and are caught,
gently.
                                              With a strange smile,
                                                  I need to be home.

My father had a second family,
I found out when I was 10 years old.
I just want to let you know this is
why I'm often distant.
                        I am curious,
what is it that you miss?
                                        Without hesitation, *the rain.*

Well, what is the difference between rain,
and what's right here between us?
Gesturing toward
                              the glass of water
                              sitting motionless
                              on the table.
                                     With quietly ruptured insides, *You*
                                     are asking me to define the difference
                                     between still water in a glass and
                              water,
                              falling,
                              from the
                              sky.
Would you like to live forever?
                                    Silence engulfs a confused expression,
                                       I don't know how to answer that question.
If you could be immortal,
would you?
                        A continued expression of silence
                                              followed by, *I'm sorry,*
                                        I just don't understand the question.

Challenges, Tempests, and Petty Annoyances

A break and a fumble
to find the closest articulation
of an inexplicable human emotion:

*I am in a constant state of feeling
trapped in this physical form.*

Gesturing toward the skin of my limbs,
pulling its walls away from my bones.

*Life is forever unending, reciprocal,
a continuous renewal of breath.*

*Death is a great illusion,
simply the moment of release,
the transcendence of these walls.*

*Birth and rebirth,
to new form, or possibly,
hopefully, formlessness.*

*I apologize for speaking in fragments,
but, would I like to be trapped
in this body for eternity?
Fuck no, absolutely not.*

With the incomplete sarcasm
of a slightly broken heart:

*I was just curious if you would be free
for coffee in two hundred years,
I suppose not.*

*Where would you like to meet?
No, no, not here, yeah, yeah,
climate change, your'e right.*

*Well somewhere
not underwater.*

*If i still happen to be in this
body when the leaves
begin to fall.*

*I will happily
meet you for coffee
in a place above the sea.*

~ **Sophia Mish**

Sofia Mish received her BFA in studio art from NYU. Sofia Mish is a self-taught poet hailing from Southeastern, PA. Mish shares a studio at GoggleWorks Center for the Arts with her creative partner Julie Stopper; the two women work together to explore the relationship between literature and visual art.

"Medusa with Theater Mask" art by Reggie Waters

Amphibian Brain

Hiss like a rattler.

Thump like a rabbit.

Snort like a deer.

The two-year-old in me, screams at the two-year-old in you.

Movement ahead.

Encroachment.

Unfamiliar scent.

The two-year-old in me, screams at the two-year-old in you.

Birds become silent.

Lady bugs fly home.

Pill bug curls into a ball.

The two-year-old in me, screams at the two-year-old in you

The wind always blows.

Clouds change shape.

Seasons progress.

Calm the child within, calm the child within.

~ Sylvia Morra

Sylvia enjoys writing haiku and other forms of poetry. Her favorite topics center on nature and religion. Mary Oliver is one of the poets that she admires.

"Odds" art by Lauralynn White

Unheard

You said
 trust me
I did
 Let's be a team
You convinced me
 I will take care of you

So I surrendered
> *Take my name*

I want to keep mine
> *I have a dream a passion*

Everything went to that
> *Let's have six boys for the farm and one girl to set the table.*

All I have is two living children
> *But I am too busy to help*

I am giving birth to a dead baby
> *It's uncomfortable, I don't know how*

Just hold me
> *Why are you so needy?*

Come play with me
> *I am not interested in what you are interested in*

Can you choose to spend more time with me?
> *I want to go hunting with the other men*

Can we vacation together as a family?
> *I am going, can you stay and help work with my family?*

Please don't leave me with two little babies and people
.... who don't understand me.
> *I do all the work, it's my money*

Can I help,
> *what I do is more important and*

Can we be partners?
> *you can't do it.*

I thought what's yours is mine and what's mine is yours.
> *Don't take MY truck.*

Let's hang out in bed; the kids are gone.
> *Why don't you want to have sex with me?*

Why don't you want to make love WITH me?
> *Stay home!*

I'm busy

~ Jillian Wright Prout

"Grab Pussy and Run" art by Susan Biebuyck

What Gives You the Right?

I scream loudly in my head
>*Because God forbid I get angry*

Look I know my place

Be sweet and smile and get along
>*Don't disrupt interrupt*

Don't have a goal or aim that would contradict the leading male in your life
>*(So choose wisely)*

But really, what gives you the right?

To touch my body?
>*It's my body*

For me

Not yours
>*For pleasure*
>
>*for fantasy*
>
>*to ogle*

Nothing

You're just some stranger on the street
>*Person I work for*
>
>*One I'm related to*

Because I've tried it all!
>*Didn't work*

So now what?

I did my part

Why can't you control your desire?

Because really!

What gives you the right?

I didn't.

You ask you to touch me

Ran your fingers under my tender little breasts

ask you to whistle

Hollered that word

ask you leer

Undressed me with your eyes

Make eye contact

Stared at me on the path

Smile at you

Approached me anyway

Look away

Stood over me, hot breath raising the hairs

Show you my ankles

Said I had a beautiful body, you wanted to own

Wear high-heeled shoes

Liked my running shoes

Wear short shorts

Found skin anyway

Get drunk

Didn't ask permission

Challenges, Tempests, and Petty Annoyances 87

Wear a long black dress

> *Would have found an excuse to take!*

Have a hair covering

> *Wrapped your fist in my ponytail*

Wear a veil

> *Shoved you're stinking lips onto my neck*

Wear my hair down showing off my shining locks in the sun

> *Yanked my hair so hard I crashed to the ground*

Lay on the cement for you

> *Fell on my body crushing the air out*

Falsely accuse you

> *Penetrated and invaded me*

Do whatever turns you on

> *Saw what you wanted*

Give you permission

> *Took*

Do it

> *DID*

~ *Jillian Wright Prout*

Due to her dyslexia, Jillian came to writing late in life. She kept a journal of thoughts but only started "putting it out there" when she joined Facebook. Jillian is a wife, a mother, a farmer, an artist, a yogini and now a writer. Her education includes a fine arts degree from Kutztown University, and 500 hours of yoga training, plus a year at DePaul University for acting. Her family moved a lot, but Lake Dunmore, Vermont, is where she called home until she and her husband bought a beautiful farm in Oley, Pennsylvania.

***"Spot On"* art by Susan Biebuyck**

Do Not Go Gentle Into Menopause
(with apologies to Dylan Thomas)

Do not go gentle into menopause.
Ladies in mid-life with emotions and bodies that burn.
Rage, rage against thy changing body.

Tho some wise women have faced this betrayal and rejoice;
I hold the hands to stop the internal clock.
I do not go gentle into menopause.

Brave women with soft flesh and furrowed brow.
Wear your high-heeled boots and cleavage proud.
Rage, rage against thy changing body.

Wild women with passion who danced and played,
Now no heads turn nor whistles heard.
Do not go gentle into menopause.

And now myself teetering on the edge.
I curse and rant against nature's clock.
I do not go gentle into menopause and
I rage, rage against thy changing body.

*~ **Ginny Rathman***

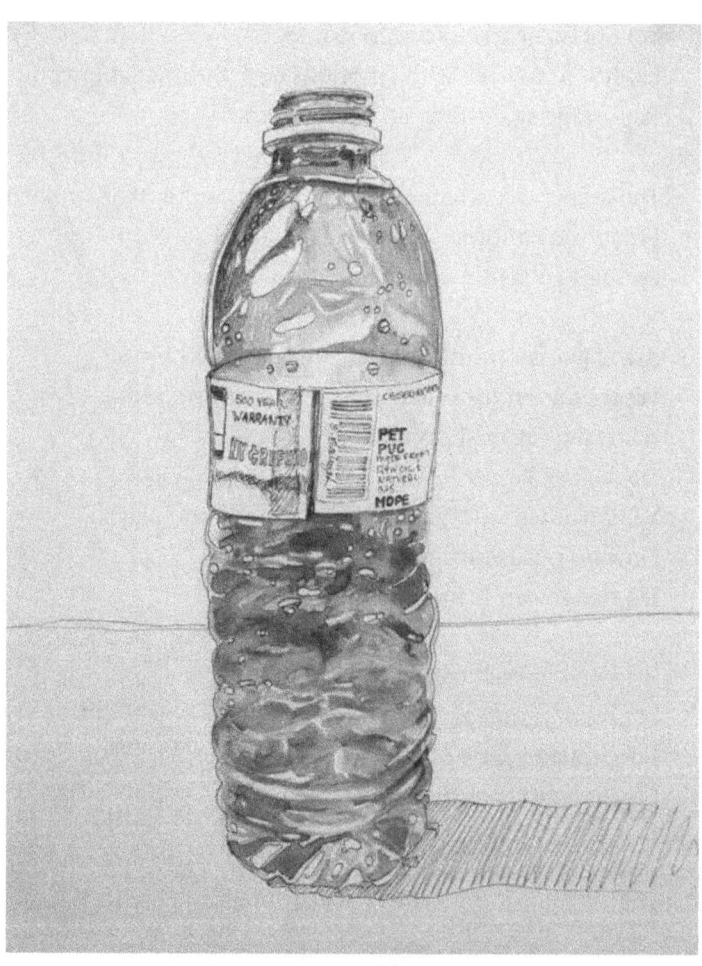

"500 Years" art by Susan Biebuyck

POLLUTER

Two abandoned old TV sets.

Eviserated VHS tapes spewing their entrails of brown shiny ribbon alongside the road.

Mattresses tossed to eventually become sinking rafts launched into the river.

Plastic bags snagged by shrubs and trees blow in the breeze while various paper products dot the landscape.

Why?

Why, you lazy piece of trash, are you shedding your disease; causing blight on my idyllic commute?

~*Ginny Rathman*

Ginny is a new-to-writing poetess who was driven to put her thoughts and feelings to paper before she feared totally losing her mind! Ginny does not know what she wants to do with her writing but hopes it resonates with all humanity.

Take a Knee

I don't care if they kneel, when the outcome reveals
That the world ought to hear when folks cry.
What I fear is the ruse, that their act tells the troops
That their service does not earn our pride.

When a man genuflects, He is showing respect
And his head rightly bows humbly down.
I reject the false claim, that a protestor shames
All the heroes with boots on the ground.

Any anthem we sing has a heart-swelling ring
For we honor the past with our song.
But if some bite their tongue, others act as if stung
By the whisper that something is wrong.

Let 'em kneel, let 'em kneel, let 'em kneel, let 'em kneel!
Though I won't wear their cause on my sleeve.
Let 'em feel, let 'em feel, let 'em feel, let 'em feel.
Let each voice declare that we believe
That the right to be heard is assured and deserved,
Far above the false flags which deceive.

When a mentor addresses his charges, they kneel.
If he makes the request for attention, they kneel.
Out of utmost respect, let the record reflect
When one feels fully humbled, he kneels.

When man asks for the holiest promise, he kneels,
In his dropping to one knee, he fully reveals
That the highest regard is an intricate part
Of the posture adopted - he kneels.
Let 'em kneel, let 'em kneel, let 'em kneel, let 'em kneel!
Though I won't wear their cause on my sleeve.
Let 'em feel, let 'em feel, let 'em feel, let 'em feel.
Let each voice declare that we believe
That the right to be heard is assured and deserved,
Far above the false flags which deceive.

It's a lie that the gesture to drop to a knee,
Is obnoxious affront to the troops overseas.
Or to any and all who keep you and I free,
When we kneel we say, "*Don't* look at me!"

Not by posture or sound may the critics expound
On the insult the action implies.
When we lower ourselves, while the hymn proudly swells,
We refute by our station the lies
That appoint disrespect to symbolic neglect.
With great reverence we cautiously rise.

Please show me a scene where to kneel may be seen
As indignant? Is deference contempt?
Is the man who withholds, or who quietly scolds
Stained with guilt, or is he held exempt?

Let 'em kneel, let 'em kneel, let 'em kneel, let 'em kneel!
Though I won't wear their cause on my sleeve.
Let 'em feel, let 'em feel, let 'em feel, let 'em feel.
Let each voice declare that we believe
That the right to be heard is assured and deserved,
Far above the false flags which deceive.
If you feel me, then please take a knee.

~ Philip Repko

Phil Repko is a career educator in the PA public school system who has been writing for fun and no profit since he was a teenager. Phil lives with his wife Julie in Gilbertsville and is the father of three outstanding children, two of whom are also poets and writers. He vacillates between poetry and prose, as the spirit beckons, and is currently working sporadically on a novella and a memoir.

CAN'T

So, you want me in public to make a rant?

I will not!

I won't.

Sorry, I just can't.

With so much about which to chant

I'm aware some would allege

As a babe I was dropped on my head,

But today I just want to be silly instead.

~ *Jay Ressler*

A native of Berks County, Jay Ressler graduated from Oley High School and Albright College. Before moving back to the area in 2014 he was active in the art scene in Pittsburgh for a number of years. Although he is now a full-time artist, during much of his working life he was at different times an underground coal miner and steelworker and active in union affairs. Ressler has a history of activism including in the civil rights and anti-Vietnam war movements.

"Locker Room" art by Mary Salen

STIRRING THE ASHES

On all sides women speak, so articulate.

Remembering events from long ago.

Those things never happened to me

I say to myself.

Yet . . . and yet . . . the stories stir shards and ashes

I thought were dead and cold.

There are embers, alive,

Burning still.

Damn. I thought these memories were dead. Or maybe hadn't

happened.

Why couldn't I find the words when I needed them?

Why couldn't I see

That predatory gleam in his eye?

That talk - so smooth,

So enticing.

Did I not have the language?

Or was it the understanding?

Or was it the will?

My older self screams NO to my younger self.

Tectonic plates are shifting beneath our feet.

This didn't happen yesterday.

But it is happening now.

Girls are growing tall and strong.

Will they have a life

That is safe and free,

Unrestricted by the wolves,

The jackals,

The foxes I knew?

~ Martha Ressler

Martha Ressler makes, teaches and tirelessly promotes art quilts, which are a creative visual work that is layered and stitched. Marty was a painter who loved to sew, so she has found her medium. She moved from Pittsburgh to Berks County 3 years ago where she has found renewed inspiration.

LOVE THEM SOCKS

Jocks wear socks.
And docs wear socks.
And artists wear them, too.

But unlike docs,
and most of the jocks,
mine aren't black or blue.

No, I wear lots
of colorful socks
under shoes or boots or Keds.

Some have dots,
some stripes or blocks
of pinks, chartreuse or reds.

My brilliant socks
bring smiles to lots
of people whom I meet.

But I most enjoy,
yes, truly enjoy
how they wrap my happy feet.

~ Dan Roberts

"Snow Day" art by Ed McCarty

The Snow Fix

Some people just know

when it's going to snow.

So they wait with hope,

like junkies outta dope,

waiting, wanting, craving

yet another fix of that white stuff

called snow.

~ Dan Roberts

Monday Morning Brew

It's Monday morning
I'm still in bed
my body aches
it feels like lead

It's cold outside
and in here, too
So what do I want?
I want my brew.

That's what I need
'cause it starts my day
it gets me goin'
sends me on my way

Dont need no sugar
Don't need no cream
Just make it hot
with plenty of steam

And I don't need no bagel
Don't need no chow
What I need is my coffee
And I need it NOW!

~ *Dan Roberts*

As a young man Dan Roberts, an artist, writer and graphic designer from West Reading, Pennsylvania, wrote an occasional poem or short story, mostly for his own pleasure. However, motivated by the passing of his wife in 2005, Dan started using writing as a therapy to overcome his loss. His present writing covers a broad range of subjects, anywhere from humor to philosophical. He has written a number of poems, several short stories and one novel that have been published.

"Getting a Kick Out of Life" art by Jim Meehan

OF POLTERGEIST AND ANTI-MATTER

How odd it is to me, how queer

that things I hold so dear

disappear!

When I am by myself

what I left on the shelf

on or my desk or table

vanishes! Were I able

to believe

I could retrieve

my precious junket or bauble

I would not dawdle

but search

and crouch

and stretch

and scoop

and stoop!

Phooey!

The black hole was hungry—

clearing

my earring

and then

my pen

or worse—

my purse

and— jeese!

my keys!

PLEASE!

Regurgitate, you other sphere,

or kindly vanish

outta here!

~ Theresa Rodriguez

Theresa Rodriguez is the author of <u>Jesus and Eros: Sonnets, Poems and Songs</u> (www.bardsinger.com).

REPERCUSSIONS

Classified by money, gripped no less
by equal-ness. cross-purposed
at our core, in knots hung there,
not knowing who to be, or where to go.

O life, liberty and the pursuit of b-s.
We are so not equal, weighed down
by infatuation with those above us.
Santayana observed this years ago.

I mention it now in the spirit of
proper attribution, so essential
when so many are getting screwed.
Marmalade head! Agent Orange! not all your fault.

You are the culmination of decades
of incestuous trafficking
between haves and have-nots, media drugged,
meaning flung aside, a useless hunk of shit.

But you understood the game, embodied
every false premise, now at your command.
A lie as good as the truth, if you can spit
them out faster than we can follow.

This visceral sense of dread. Fearful innocence
in nefarious times. Justice a foundling
in the cold. Scar tissue covers old wounds
but not new ones. Words adhere to facts

and plot remorseless vengeance.

~ Michael Schiffman

"99 Elephants A Day" art by Suzanne Fellows

Dismay at the Grocery Store

I dip my pen in sour ink
and write of hatred, hatred I say,
for that Giant supermarket chain,
that pygmy, that hermaphroditic
place, where all of us mutate
into a single sex, selfsame, infertile, lost.

I arrive disgruntled, depart in fury.
They insist on moving the garlic,
the avocados, the spinach--
now in two places, the better deal
off by itself. And the canned, organic
low sodium beans now hide where they've
never been before. And all the little,
pointless stack outs that clog the aisles:
salty snacks of every kind,
and sweets angled to funnel children
into their path. Poor parents, broken
on the wheel of that impulse sale.

All of this makes my blood boil.
I've never seen a manager,
some guy with a tie actually
working, Only the lower level
gals are exposed to the public,
doing whatever they do,
And the grunts who make the place run?
They rarely stack the shelves.
or they'll fill them with the wrong.
items. Price tags are moot. I've seen
them dump unripe fruit on top of ripe
or pre-bagged produce into
the fresh veggie bin. They all

have that robotic, moronic
look of the alienated,
the disengaged. Pure anomie.
And where is a sociologist
when you need one? Answer me that,
you pusillanimous bunch of shoppers!

They don't even give us a few pennies
back for the bags they ask you to bring
help the environment. Like they care.
I'd rather live with elephants, sensible
creatures who don't throw their weight around.
They're being driven to extinction.
I'll cast my lot with them. Are you with me?

~ Michael Schiffman

Michael Schiffman retired five years ago after a three-part career as a wine salesman, businessman, and eternal student. His interest in poetry goes back almost fifty years, and he started writing in earnest over ten years ago. He lives in an 1800 brick federal home in downtown Reading, the city where he was born and a source, perversely or not, of much inspiration. His work has appeared in "These Fragile Lilacs," Step Away magazine, and Rise, an anthology of poetry on work and justice from Vagabond Books.

Twelver

Me and Tim was sitting at his parent's house reading comic books, scary ones, like, you know, <u>Creepy</u>, <u>Eerie</u>, really cool shit. I was twelve, so was Tim, and we loved those scary black and white comics. My parents, more my dad, cuz mom didn't care, didn't want me reading them because he thought they were a bad influence on me, so I'd sneak off to my buddy's place after we'd get one and read them in his place.

Both his parents worked, so we never had a problem with them telling us what to do. He did have an older brother that was in charge. He never stuck around us because we were too young for him and he didn't like hanging around with twelvers, as he called us. Of course that didn't bother us, because we didn't like hanging around with him either, he was kind of a dick, and not very nice. Besides, next year we'd be thirteeners and he was too fuckin' lazy to say an extra syllable. We knew it. He always liked to play jokes on us, boss us around and call us names like we were inferior pieces of shit to him.

But man, the latest <u>Eerie</u> magazine was awesome, the stories were spooky as shit, and we were really getting into it. I was reading a story called "The Damned Thing" for the fourth time when all of a sudden Tim's brother ran out of the bedroom with a double barrel shotgun. He stopped right in front of me and aimed it in my face where I could see down the barrel of the gun. He said, "You're dead, motherfucker!"

I pissed myself, couldn't help it. He pulled the dual trigger and the gun went ... click-click.

Nothin' happened, there was nothin' in the gun, but I didn't know. I started crying and couldn't stop. I was shaking. He laughed, the prick, thought it was real funny, had a good laugh over it, and so did his brother, Tim, my buddy.

I got so mad I jumped up and punched him hard in the jaw. I hurt my hand. I called him a fucking asshole. He seemed surprised, like

I shouldn't hit him or say that. I didn't hurt him, he was bigger and stronger than me.

He rubbed his jaw and said, "I was only joking, fucker." But it wasn't a joke to me. I knew what a shotgun was and if there were real bullets in the gun I'd be dead. It happens that kids kill someone or themselves just by fuckin' around.

"Did you fucking piss yourself, you fucking pussy?" Tim said, looking at my crotch, and his brother started laughing again, saying, "Yeah man, and he's fucking crying too!" I was still shaking. I thought I could have died if the gun was loaded. I knew then that neither of these ass-warts were a friend to me no more, so I picked up my magazine and left without saying a word.

"Don't drip on my parent's rug," Tim said.

I walked back to my house and my mom was home. I put the comic in front of my jeans so she wouldn't see the piss stain. Noticing that something was wrong she said "Are you okay, honey?" But I just shrugged. She saw the magazine and said, "You better put that away before your father sees it." I went to my room, hid the book and washed up.

The next day Tim called to get together like nothing happened and I told him not to ever call again because he was no longer my friend, and then I hung up on him. It didn't seem to bother him. A few days later I heard his brother shot a hole through the couch and wall.

~ Ron Schira

Ron Schira lives in Reading and for the past 23 years has been the lead art critic for the <u>Reading Eagle</u> newspaper and an individual exhibiting artist since the mid-seventies. He has had over thirty solo displays in Berks and Lehigh Counties. He writes poetry and short stories on art and other cultural topics.

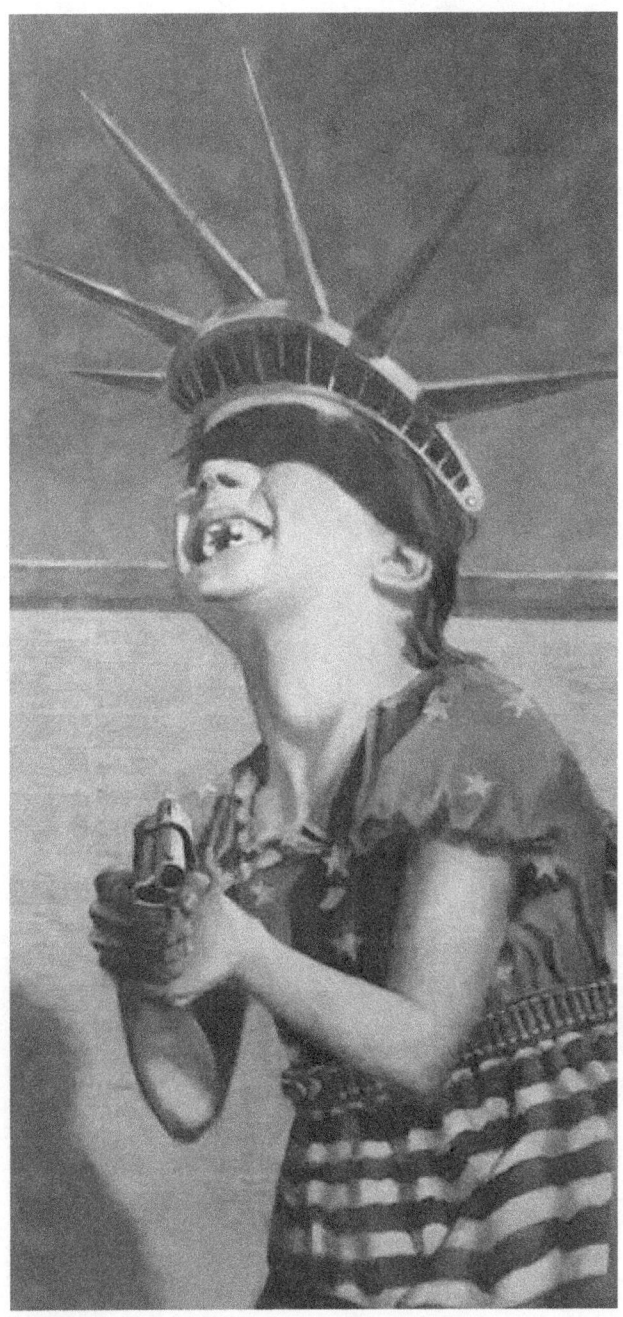

"A Well-regulated Militia" art by Charley Farrell

"2130 Wightman St. No. 27" art by Erika Stearly

Challenges, Tempests, and Petty Annoyances

TO MY BROTHER

So young you were...

I remember.

You couldn't reach it.

Mommy said it was okay

To lay it on the floor.

But now you're as tall as me

And I still get my socks wet

From your damp towels

On the bathroom floor.

~ *Amy Stahl*

Amy is a free spirit, an intuitive empath, a true Gemini, negotiating her current incarnation among us as patiently as she can. In high school her talents in video production earned awards. Caretaking became her most recent role. Basset hounds capture her heart.

"Fake Art" by Big Dutch Dave Nally

WE ALL SUFFER THE SAME*

Boyertown, PA. In a surprise announcement, Paul D. Stahl, 70, announced his candidacy for President 2020, adopting as his campaign slogan, "We All Suffer the Same."

"Paul has pledged to break the back of partisan politics now rampant in all levels of government and within the nation's constituency," explained Nicole Johnson, 37, his campaign manager and niece.

"Paul insists that we've got to stop seeing two sides," Johnson explained. "We have big problems to solve; but instead of focusing on the solutions to our problems, we're concerned about our political party, our personal bank account, and our own family and friends," she continued.

"Candidate Stahl is adamant that this partisan way of governing is not sustainable," she continued. "He is haunted by Nikita Khrushchev's prediction: 'We will bury you.... Your own working class will bury you.'"

"Paul recognizes that we're all in this mess together and somehow we must figure things out together. The country is destroying itself from within, and, he figures, we have 9 more years until the economy...and the nation itself...go 'belly up.'"

Pressed for additional details, Johnson deferred, promising that Stahl himself would be open for interviews, but she offered that the #1 plank in his platform is to institute a law calling for capital punishment for driving in the left lane when not passing another vehicle.

"There will be no second chances or appeals," Johnson explained. "If convicted, the penalty is death. Paul did suggest that he'd allow you to choose your preferred method, however."

"His rationale is quite logical," Johnson explained, "and based around the need to 'trim the herd' of the greediest, least empathic in our society who feel entitled to have and do whatever they want. In a word, he is eager to build a society of team players."

"Candidate Stahl is certain that those who feel entitled to drive in the left lane may include those who deny others a living wage, affordable health insurance, and food for Fluffy. Logically, then, as we administer the consequences of the Left Lane Law, we'll be left without those who think the world owes them whatever they like. They'll all be dead."

"Another plank that speaks to building a society of team players would include re-instituting the draft for all 18-year-olds. The 'draft' would be a mandatory two-year community service of some kind, not just military," she continued.

"But central to the individual's service would be 'breaking' the individual ego and encouraging a team-centered way of living," she noted. "There will be no special favors or extenuating circumstances. His plan, stated in his campaign slogan, is simple: we all must suffer the same because pain is instructive, humbling, and will build the character this country needs to survive."

*Fake news

~ *Jane Stahl*

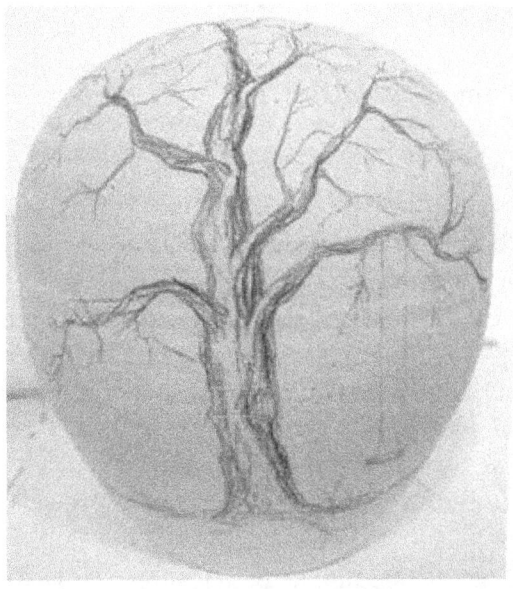

"Thinking Tree" art by Linda Rohrbach-Austerberry

A Wish List for Our Time

~ *Quoted passages from Lawrence Ferlinghetti, "Christ Climbed Down," A Coney Island of the Mind, 1958*

"Christ climbed down
from His bare Tree
this year
and ran away to where
there were ..."

no pussy-grabbing Presidents,
no Rocket Men with fragile egos,
no Confederate flags boasting supremacy,
and no walls erected to keep us from our friends.

"Christ climbed down

*from his bare Tree
this year
and ran away to where..."*

every one who suffered was offered help, not blame.
every sickness was treated without a fortune's price tag
every blessed being—cat, dog, and parakeet—could count on kindness, not neglect
and every talent or skill was appreciated all the same.

*"Christ climbed down
from his bare Tree
this year
and ran away to where..."*

folks believed one another because everyone honored truth,
folks recognized they were not entitled to take advantage,
folks knew that working together made work light,
and that sarcasm ruined relationships and sparked resentment and cold rage.

Christ said he didn't care about gilded Christmas trees, or tinsel, or tinfoil.
He said that pink plastic was as good as gold or black or even powder blue.

He likes electric candles—even LED's
and tin electric trains are fun for kids and cornball relatives.
He loves them all.

*"Christ climbed down
from His bare Tree
this year
and ran away to where..."*

Bible salesmen shared coffee with the Buddha,
Mohammed was invited to dinner,
and those of no religion enjoyed the same respect.

*"Christ climbed down
from his bare Tree
this year
and ran away to where..."*

His birthday was celebrated with hugs,
and tugs were only done in fun.
Fat Santas in red flannel suits and fake white beards
hummed "Winter Wonderland" and
fed the reindeer cookies and milk.

*"Christ climbed down
from His bare Tree
this year
and softly stole away into
some anonymous Mary's womb again
where in the darkest night
of everybody's anonymous soul
He awaits again
an unimaginable
and impossibly
Immaculate Reconception
the very craziest
of Second Comings"*

~*Jane Stahl*

Jane Stahl currently serves as Director of Community Relations for Studio B following 35 years of sharing a love of literature, writing, and speaking with junior high and high school students and a love of teaching with fellow teachers and the community. Following their dream of living in an artistic community, Jane and her husband Paul founded Boyertown's Bear Fever community art project that ultimately led her into collaboration with fine artist Susan Biebuyck and the establishment of Studio B. So many projects, so little time! Jane hopes someday to take the time to self-publish a collection of her thoughts and experiences.

"None of Your Damn Business" art by Charley Farrell

Death by Apologetics

Strung up in public
His thoughts penned
on billboards that bear
his name and resemblance
A family forsaken by
expectation and reluctant stares
Bland pages stamped
with opinions, too opaque
for light additions of words.
Complications of advancement
brought on by a meaningless
definition of how and why.

Who am I to judge?
Who are they at all?
I love them as I love myself.
Please tell me who I am,
so I can open my heart to you.
Blank pages and apologies
Brought down by tears and thunder
Burn through, my Sun!
Bring me my heat and life
Remember me, child,
as you remember your soul
Your past has passed, give
it away to the present.

Day sells itself to the
night for another cigarette
Can you hear me anymore?
Can you see without your
ears and words?
Come from me without fear.
Go for a walk with your angels.
"She will bring you back to me," He said
And in time, I will tell you
why I haven't told you before
I will tell you soon
All will be revealed

You can handle it.
You've gotta take it
Bring them with you
You'll need them along the way
Bring water to the river

~ J.D. Stahl

J.D. loathes labels, but in this "go-round" of his many lives he's a teacher, a life coach, a musician, and lover of language. Challenging accepted norms, led by logic and love and an eternal quest for truth, J.D. infuses good intentions toward the recovery and self-discovery of those whose life paths cross his own. For his own evolution, J.D. is constantly seeking ascension towards universal concepts and answers encompassing this world and the next. His own mentor is his beloved canine Ginger.

Challenges, Tempests, and Petty Annoyances

"#<3" photo courtesy of Ginger Stahl

"Take Out - Wednesday" art by Kristen Woodward

UGH!

Our earth has always had some forms of pollution. Back on early earth, there were dust storms, volcanic activity, animal wastes, and animal methane or decay. I'm not sure how tough this was for cavemen or dinosaurs, but the world we live in now has some form of dangerous pollution everywhere you go. Modern man and his "civilization" are responsible for the thousand-fold increase.

Man's first waste was probably sewage. For years we just dumped it in the ground and waterways. We took a big step in figuring out how to treat our own waste, not realizing it was still poorly regulated. Our waste water has detergents, chemicals, and pharmaceuticals (Yeah, all our drugs and medicines.) Most of that crap sneaks through the treatment process, going right back to the environment and its living creatures. Studies have shown insects and fish have birth defects, cell abnormalities, and even behavioral problems. Small amounts of anti-depressants have been shown to cause fish not to travel in schools and occasionally become untypically aggressive!

Our next waste was probably garbage. For years we just dumped it or buried it. Oh, and we liked to burn it too! Now we've got humongous landfills that leak pollution and we're still dumping in the waterways. In the ocean there are floating garbage islands, one the size of Texas, getting bigger everyday. Did I mention we still like to burn it!

Next we needed to get from one place to another faster. Enter the internal combustion engine! Yes, that wonderful advancement, bringing us V.O.C. fumes, lead particulate, black carbon particulate, carbon monoxide, asbestos dust, etc., etc., etc.

Oh! Then we needed to keep warm, keep cool, and have power for all of our gadgets, etc. etc. etc. Now we have created this air, water, and land stew of waste and chemicals. It's gotten so bad, the best we can do is try to figure out what are safe levels we can tolerate. Domestic waste, sewage, coastal marine dumping, radioactive waste, oil, plastics, sulfur dioxide, carbon monoxide, nitrogen oxide, lead, zinc, mercury, detergents, pesticides, herbicides, CFC's, benzene, PVC, PCB, BPA, hospital wastes, formaldehyde, asbestos, pharmaceuticals, fluorides, RF fields, electromagnetic fields, etc., etc., etc.

Industrialized asthma, heart disease, toxin poisoning, lung disease, and cancer are the by-products of our progress. There is less and less natural water suitable to drink. There are many rivers that are now too polluted to support life, land too polluted to support farming, cities too polluted to support breathing, and our oceans are getting fished out and dumped in! Ah yes, we've come a long way!

~ *Burton Stehly*

5PPM

Got it in the air,
got it in the ground
No hiding place,
it can't be found

Better living now,
through chemistry
Getting rid of it,
they did not foresee

Got the water laced,
pumped it in the air
There's a measured trace,
hidden everywhere

Stuff you can't pronounce,
in a toxic mess
What are safe amounts?
anybody's guess

Somethin like 5 parts per million
Somethin like 5 parts per billion

Barrels in the ground,
pourin out the stacks
Clouding air and water,
clouding up the facts

PCB, DDT,
BPA, killin me?
Herbicide, pesticide
suicide, nationwide!

~ *Burton Stehly*

In the late 80's and early 90's Burton Stehly was the lyricist-poet for the experimental industrial group "Slavekind." In his travels he met the world renowned electronic instrument designer, Phillip Cirocco; Arizona avante-garde jazz bassist, Gary Evans; and Michael Macdonald, former drummer of the group "Gene Loves Jezebel" from Scotland. This became the touring group "National Razor." Burton was lyricist for their four subsequent album releases. He also continued live reading performances. He was never content to write strictly about personal feelings although it was a great self-therapy. Consequentially, he turned from inward to outward on the many lessons and pathways in the world he was traveling. His latest endeavor is a collection of writings in his book entitled <u>Beauty Among Thorns</u>, available through Create Space or by contacting him the1burton@yahoo.com

"Searching for a Sign" art by Charley Farrell

CAN I GET A WITNESS

Can I get a witness to agree
That we hold these truths to be self-evident
That all men are created equal and
Have certain inalienable rights, among them
Life, liberty and the pursuit of happiness

Can I get a witness to agree
That we have spent
The last 241 years learning nothing

Can I get a witness to agree
That the ideas being fostered in this country
Today are wrong

Can I get a witness to agree
That the sale of military grade weapons
To the general public has to stop

Can I get a witness to agree
That it's harder to buy allergy pills
Than to buy crack on any street corner

Can I get a witness to agree
That big industry and big money
Run this country
Not we the people

Can I get a witness to agree
That politicians are more concerned about themselves
Than their constituents or this country

Can I get a witness to agree
That it's time to abolish the electoral college,

Lobbyists and special interest groups
And to limit elected officials to two terms
Eliminating career politicians

Can I get a witness to agree
That apathy is a major problem
In this country

Can I get a witness to agree
That we are our own worst enemy
And that common sense is as hard to find
As a virgin in a whorehouse

~ *R.H. Strauss*

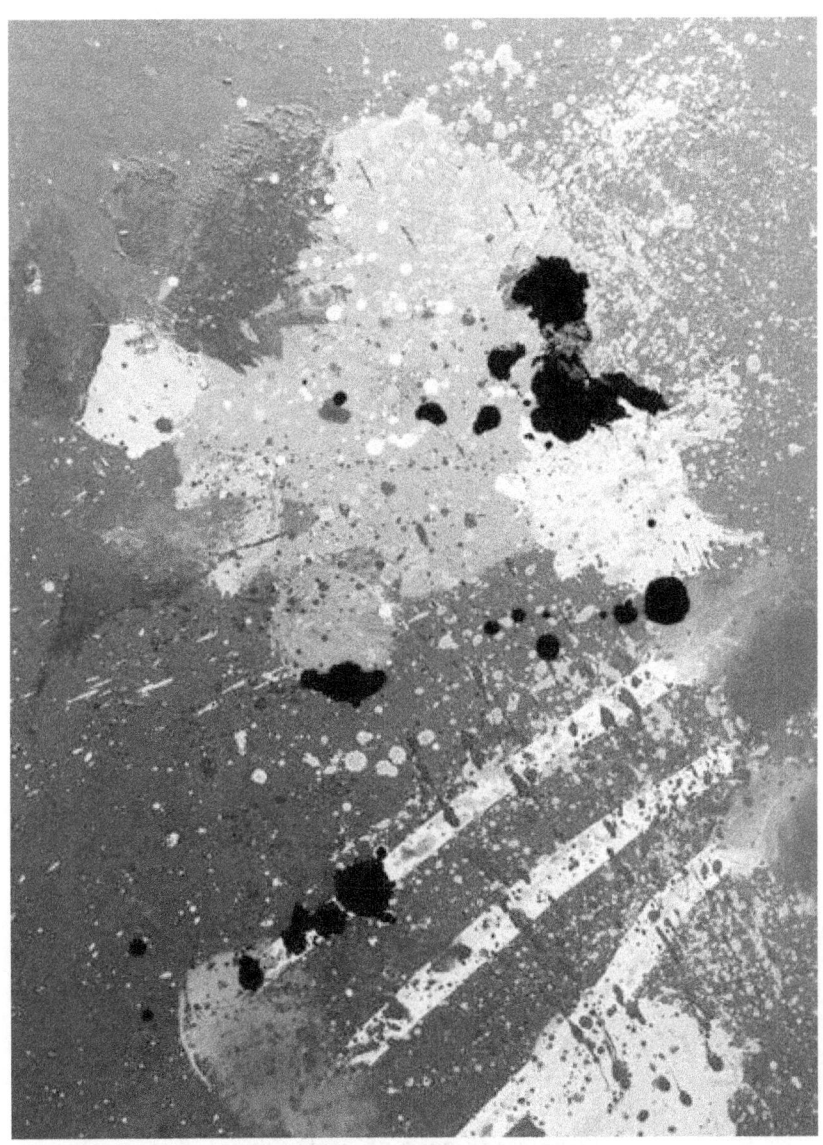

"I Heard You the First Time" **art by Suzanne Fellows**

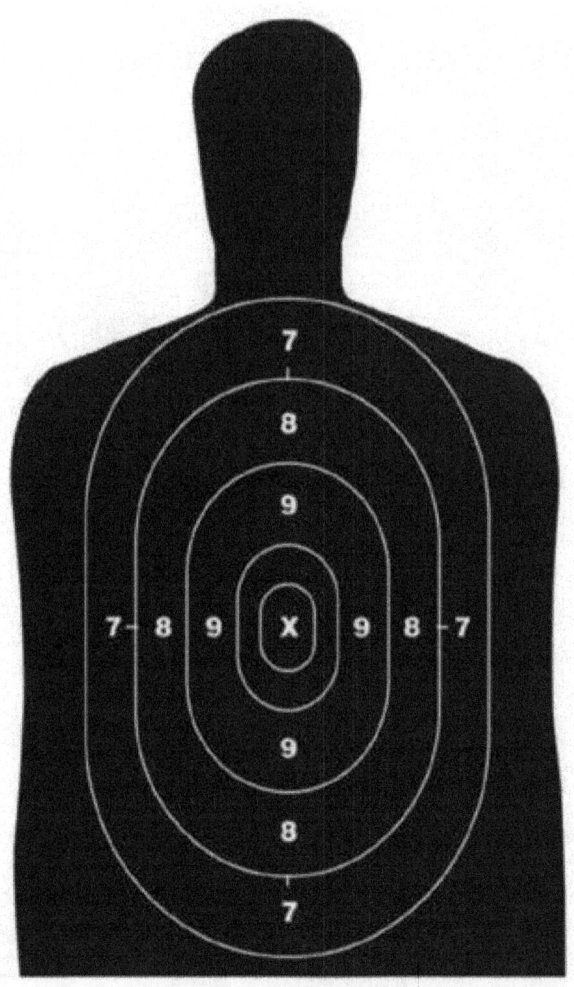

"Targeted" art by Sue DaNym

TIRED OF BEING

It happens I'm tired of being
White and worrying that my
Next words might, somehow
Sound racially charged

It happens I'm tired of being
White and considered to be
Only interested in myself

It happens I'm tired of being
White and part of the
White power structure just
Because I am white
The same way a black man
Is considered a criminal just
Because he is black

~ R.H. Strauss

Rod has written poetry and short stories for 54 years. He's divorced; proud father of 2 fantastic sons; member of Berks Bards and Pagoda Writers; retired and enjoying it; a published poet who has performed on stage, at coffee shops in the 1970's and on TV and film.

Art by Theodore R. Thomas

The Four Stages of a Woman's Life Expressed as Bakery Goods

Cookies

The variety of shapes, sizes and taste of cookies excites the boyhood senses and is never forgotten. All the more because the discovery and capture of a cookie has the added excitement of stealth: snatching it warm and fresh from the kitchen, concealing it until it can be consumed in a secret place far from adult eyes. No boy ever forgets his first cookie, when hunger was great, time was short and bites were huge.

Cupcakes

In adulthood, cookies become cupcakes. Softer, plumper and contained in form fitting wrappers, the cupcake is more demanding and far more rewarding than a cookie. One takes one's time savoring a cupcake after carefully removing its baked-on wrapper to retain the mood and texture of the moment. Cupcakes are enjoyed in adult, civilized settings with comfortable upholstery, adequate heating and often with the pleasure enhancement of a warm drink. The lifespan of a cupcake is entirely unpredictable. Some never reach middle age; others, with proper frosting, endure as consumable delicacies into old age.

Biscuits

Biscuits are the warm, nourishing fare of late middle age. Prepared in aromatic settings and presented on a table decorated with a box of breakfast cereal and a bottle of multi-vitamins. But biscuits require careful handling. They must be lovingly buttered, then jams, jellies and other confections applied for taste. Their light, soft texture is fragile. It lasts but a little while; and if left alone without warmth or butter, a biscuit becomes hardened and stale.

Scones

An unfortunate few biscuits survive to become scones. A scone is better displayed than enjoyed. Usually found only in the company of other scones, it is served with strong, scalding tea on little lace doilies. It takes considerable courage to approach a scone, as both the exterior crust and interior nuttiness are daunting.

~ Theodore R. Thomas

Art by Theodore R. Thomas

DEATH OF TRUST

That high tech bubble that burst spectacularly in 2000 was a faded memory in the fall of 2007. Exuberance had returned. "The market is transparent," screamed financial advisors from their desks in shopping malls and high rise offices. "We have new controls, new rules, assurance of open and honest dealings," the experts say. New brokers and analysts? "Well, no, but the old ones have reformed; see for yourself: the DOW is approaching all time highs. It didn't get that way being wrong." So went the chant.

It took about a week to lose the wealth accumulated over 8 years.

Common stocks lost roughly half their value. It had a name, this new bonfire of the vanities. They called it the Great Recession.

It was trust that died in 2007 taking deception and arrogance along with it. This time the casualties had names: Bear Sterns, Lehman Bros, Merrill Lynch.

And, of course, there are those millions of prudent, thoughtful private investors, the nameless men and women with their IRA's entrusted to financial advisors.

~ Theodore R. Thomas

Theodore Thomas, retired engineering executive and Korean War veteran, traveled the world sketching, writing, and photographing his experiences over a working lifetime, drawing inspiration to create a body of pastel paintings that preserve his memories. Some have historical importance.

"Hearts and Leaves" art by Jillian Wright-Prout

Not Quite Finished

I really have a thing against single lines of poetry that would be better broken into two

but even worse is when the poet thinks it's ingenious
to leave out one little

~ Joanne Van Wie

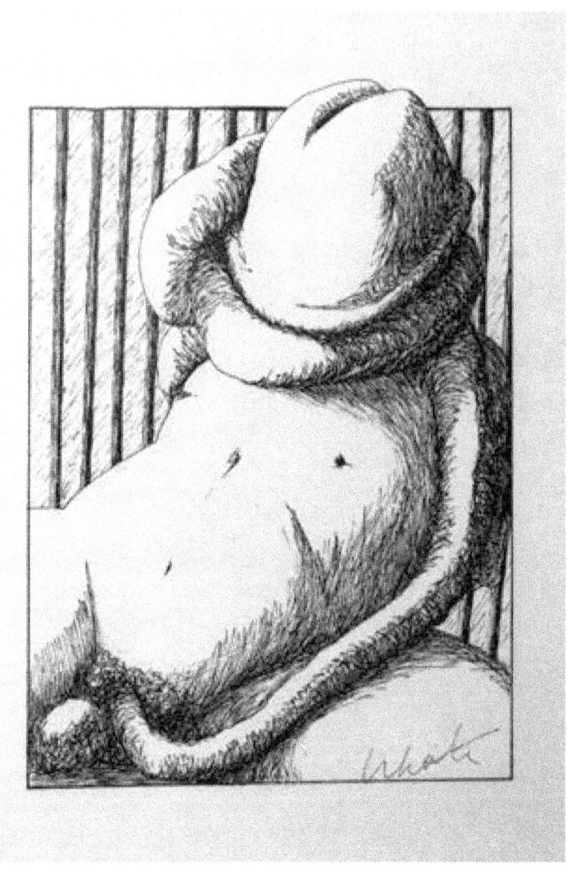

"Me Too" art by Lauralynn White

This I Know

This I know:
For the poet that rants about static in winter, or mice in the walls
or the bobbin that eternally needs rewound,
this is not my problem.
Mine is the boundary, the moment that looms
and the hour that always arrives too soon
and the way I fail to prepare, to produce.

I have loved in days unsurrounded by closets and
the closing of doors,
I have caressed the long-burning embers,
I have listened to walls that wanted to speak
but never again shall I be in this moment.

This poem could never be about the way a marriage falls apart...
there was so little time left.

~ Joanne Van Wie

Joanne Van Wie is a poet from southern Maryland whose poetry can be found in the Connections *magazine of the College of Southern Maryland and* TEXTure *magazine of Annapolis. Margaret Atwood has been her inspiration since early in her writing career. She is always pushing a deadline.*

"Frenchie Kisses" digital art by Sue DaNym

WATCH YOUR BEST FRIENDS

For most people, dogs are friends. For runners, however, they may or may not be so friendly.

As a preface, I just want to say I love dogs, particularly our golden retriever, who was a loving, caring member of our family for six short years. When I would come home, he was the first one to greet me, wiggling with excitement and smiling with his pink tongue hanging out of the one side of his mouth. I can't tell you how much I missed that warm greeting after cancer took him away from us.

Despite being a wonderful part of our family, we did not let Sparky walk with us without a leash or play in the yard unattended, even though we had an invisible electric fence. While he never hurt us or anyone, he would protect us if he thought something would harm us.

So, when I go running in the evening wearing black leggings and carrying a flashlight, I expect dogs to bark, growl or even chase me, because that's what my dog would have done. This is why it is so important for people to keep their dogs on leashes and have fences. Even if they do have a fence, they should still be aware of what their dogs are doing outside.

Unfortunately, that's not what most dog owners do. Usually, the dogs are alone and come charging at me – causing me to panic or even freeze in fear. If the owners are outside, many lamely try to call their dogs or will say, "Don't worry, she won't hurt you." Really? Do I need to find out?

One time, an unleashed dog started following me as I was running and wouldn't stop. I had no idea where he belonged. No one was visibly outside anywhere. I didn't even see a house with a light on. I backtracked to where he started following me, hoping someone would be looking for him. No. Eventually, he became more interested in sniffing a nearby garbage bag and stopped following me. I hope he made it home safely.

So, on behalf of runners, bicyclists and walkers everywhere, please be a responsible dog owner! Keep your dog in your yard in a fence or on a leash and don't let the dog outside alone. Thank you!

~ Diane VanDyke

Whether she is writing a journal entry or an article for a local newspaper, Diane VanDyke finds her creative zone when she connects words and phrases to paint a lasting image and tell a good story. Her writing adventures started in her teenage years, but then were put aside and rediscovered a decade later when she started freelance writing for her hometown newspaper. Her freelance assignments led to a part-time staff position and then to a full-time editorial position. Eventually, she followed the path of marketing and public relations, where she uses her writing skills today. Beyond writing, Diane likes to garden, hike, jog, read, ride bike, and enjoy the beauty of sunrises and sunsets.

OF THE MAKING OF MANY BOOKS

I was working on a book again this past summer.

My secretary knew that. Every other day, she would get a sheaf of almost illegibly handwritten pages which she put into clear and solid lines of type.

My family knew that too. My study door was shut from 7 a.m. until about noon each day. Breakfast and lunch were brought in. My temperament, in keeping with the progress of the manuscript, ranged from exhilaration to profound depression. My children could tell when I had what Eugene O'Neill marked on his calendar as a c.w.d., a creative working day. Is it strange that most authors, when they finally write their prefaces at the end of their labor, so frequently dedicate their work to their long-suffering families?

The process of writing a book, someone has said, is the closest metaphorical experience one can have to bringing a child into the world. The conception of the book is a seed of an idea, a glint in the eye, a possibility that may become fertile. There is the excitement of the beginning, the sketching out of an idea which always brings some unexpected insights and connections. The seed must then be in gestation; it must be gently and patiently nourished.

Then comes the actual birth, the bringing of the idea into the world. The labor pains are often excruciating. I remember

Hemingway said that he wrote and rewrote the ending of A Farewell to Arms, the last page, thirty-nine times. "Why?" asked the Paris Review questioner: "Was there some technical problem there? What was it that stumped you?" Hemingway's replay: "Getting the words right." Or, I recall Christopher Fry's response to critics who spoke of his rich ad exuberant verse as if he were verbally intoxicated; he insisted the process of writing was "more like a slow death by ground glass."

Some books are born easily. A little book on laughter I wrote several years ago in a quick month. Others are prolonged almost beyond human endurance—can one be in labor for two years? I thought—it may sound silly now, but I sometimes thought neither I nor my first book would ever live through it. I could feel myself drifting into the unknown. I scarcely hoped that I should ever be able, even for a moment, to look on the face of my little first-born. Then, when I finally saw the frail red morsel, so feeble, so infinitely pitiful, only eight inches by five and weighing about six ounces, I scarcely knew whether to be glad for myself or sorry for it. Yet very soon, I got to know every line in its dear little form, every tiny nuance and accent.

It was my child. To critics who misunderstood it and did not see its true nature, I was a touchy as could be. I would react as if they had made a disparaging remark about one of my own offspring. If a review was flattering, I would bask in the reflected light just as a proud parent does. But most of all, I was not in control anymore. Its flaws and its strengths were of my making, I knew, but I could not redo the past. It had its own life. Years later, when a ruthless publisher starved it to death—I mean let it go out of print—something died within me.

And why, pray tell, does one write another book? Not for money. Except for the few best-sellers and for textbooks, the royalties hardly pay for the typing. Not for fame, I think, although one knows some books are published in academia in order to secure enough fame to prevent perishing. Why? For learning, for growth. How do I know what I know unless I have it clearly on paper? How better to have others share with me their response to my thinking? The joy of discovery is ever new.

Why write another book? For some of the same reasons one has another child. Admittedly, sometimes that is for the purpose of improving on the last offspring, with guilt pervasively present. Mostly, however, for the wonder of the combination of the tremendously bewildering human effort completely enmeshed with inexplicable spiritual grace beyond my deserving. To write a book is to catch a faint glimpse of how God's presence begins and ends is impossible. Instead, I accept that astonishing and mysterious given. I have learned that lesson again this summer, the hard way, the only way.

~ *Nelvin Vos*

Nelvin Vos is Emeritus Professor of English at Muhlenberg College where he served for 35 years on the faculty and as Vice President and Dean of the College. He has published widely, including some dozen books ranging from <u>For God Sake's Laugh</u>, to his most recent, <u>Inter-Actions: Relationships Of Religion and Drama</u>. He and his wife Beverly have enjoyed their 18th-century stone home in east Berks County for almost 50 years.

"Mala Beads" art by Sue DaNym

JAPA

"If there had been only one Buddhist in the woodpile,"
the cynical idealist, realist poet of the people once asked
after the tragedy in Waco.

Substitute all senseless, absurdity of violence before then
until now and way beyond tomorrow.

ISIS took the name of the Egyptian mother goddess, protector of all
perverted it to their purpose
She could not save the children, Christians, Yazidi, Sunni, or
four young men whose own mothers could not protect them.

Could any power have?
It didn't; it hasn't' it couldn't

Only consciousness can—not Bodhisattva consciousness
But the tiniest bit of wonder before the infinite universe.
A modest intimation of the true human spirit
One glimpse of beauty and goodness of life and love
compassion for the other--

For just one moment
A glimmer of consciousness might have asked:

"What do I want to bring into being, to experience?"
Supreme power over everything and everyone?
Shedding blood of innocents, the arrogance of zeal?

Men of war have ever said thus:

"We will assert power over the innocents, the weak, the helpless
through terror, torture, rape and murder
wearing black masks to cover our faces of defiance

speaking threats with stone cold hearts."

Such is the history of the world—a nightmare
from which we are trying to awaken

What will the warriors rule over—
these modern hoards at the gates of civilization?
Chaos and devastation—keeping watch
lest the same thing befall them
born of the pain and malice they engendered in others.

And the nations' military deus ex machina descends upon them

While the Buddhist and we wait and meditate in the woodpile
Clapping one hand

~Sandra Williams

UNTITLED

Edging into mood, mind, my Self--unawares
creates color, chaos, confusion
indigo, apprehension of a fall, split-screen identity
What do I desire, remember, know, believe--
through distractions like a thousand tiny pearls
strung earth to sky?

~Sandra Williams

FINALLY

And I said I wouldn't complain

The cold winter in my bones ached
The coming of darkness every evening closed my heart
Then—endless rain, and more cold
Why?

I used to wonder what purpose my life served
How vain and small such musings seem to me
As I move more slowly now—even in the warmth
I wonder less often
As I become the dullness of winter—the fullness of summer

Finally, the sun—warm and golden
New leaves—tender on greening branches

Two things keep me from sadness:
The small pink, perfect cherry blossoms
Each year they appear—pure and fragrant
and
The sun's arc moving toward the mid-summer sky.

~Sandra Williams

Sandra taught world literature and writing at both the high school and higher education levels since earning a BA in English and Secondary Education at Ursinus College and an MA in English at Villanova University. She is a writer of poetry, essays and short stories, with several published articles in New View magazine UK. She has facilitated writing groups at Studio B. She is now associated with Gloucester Writers Center in Massachusetts where she facilitates a Poetry Group and is a member of the Board Education Committee. She is the author of a historical novella Moss on Stone and a Time and Tide: a collection of tales. www.cosmicseanotes.blogspot.com.

"Tech Vanitas: Blue Typewriter" photograph by Jeanette May

Revenge of the Analog
(a personal rant)

ANALOG-*relating to or using signals or information represented by a continuously variable physical quantity such as spatial position or voltage.*

Since my retirement from teaching (1998) I have done a bit of writing. However, I would not have written a paragraph, a sentence, a word, without a—as we used to call it—"word processor."

Writing on a typewriter, *oy vey*. Are you old enough to remember erasable bond typing paper and white-out. Writing without spell check, for me—impossible; and Google is magic—just magic.

Now, that said, let me also say hooray for analog! The ying to digital's yang. Outside of the screen, reality is, after all, analog. Nothing is entirely black nor white but some shade of grey.

I never bought into the fantasy that digital would make everything (or anything) better. After all, nothing in nature, which is to say in reality, is wholly black or white. In nature the switch is never on or off, but somewhere in between. Everything is a metaphorical grey. It may be toward the dark side of the scale or the opposite; but never totally black or white—never at the terminus of the scale of variables. Never 1 or 0.

Honestly, immersed in screens as we are, are we as a nation, community, family any happier, more content, leading richer more satisfying lives since the digital revolution supplanted print culture?

Digital tech is, of course, the very best at mundane tasks: keeping track of inventory or tracking your Amazon shipment; controlling the lathe or monitoring the assembly line. But pushed beyond these useful quotidian tasks the thing had turned more pernicious and invasive.

Despite people's love affair with smart phones and all things digital, any screen device is, after all, just an interactive television. For better or worse, screen culture began supplanting print culture with the advent of TV in the early 1950's. At first pundits called TV "radio with pictures," but how wrong they were. Children of that decade began sitting passively while sense and sensibility were messaged and sculpted in an electronic breeze. The appeal of TV was irresistible and vaguely addictive; an "electro-drug," I've heard it called.

It must be admitted that in our age, screen culture created in many respects a different planet peopled with a new species of human primate. Like plants bending toward the light, brain neurons grow in the direction of use, and daily immersion in the screen grows in users a different mental architecture than otherwise would develop.

It's not by chance, then, that when the first generation of children raised on TV (born in the early 50's) got to college it was 1968 and recreational drugs were "discovered." Youngsters of the 60's had been, since birth, stoned on TV.

Such is the power of personal screen stimulation to attract attention that if TV is an "electro-drug" then the internet and all its permutations can be likened a bit to crystal meth and crack cocaine. It does you, baby! Deprive an addict of his dope or deprive a teen of her phone—same thing. But we love and need our phones….

However, all the weather is not necessarily sunny in virtualville. A recent article in the Sunday NY Times by David Sax observes: "This publishing season is flush with books raising alarms about digital technology's pernicious effects on our lives: what smart phones are doing to our children; how Facebook and Twitter are eroding our democratic institutions; and the effects of tech monopolies."

And what to say then to Facebook, Twitter, and all the rest of social media? No doubt a boon to separated families and service people stationed in foreign lands, but here at home I've noticed more and more people doing less and less of it. After all, what's the point?

Challenges, Tempests, and Petty Annoyances   155

However, to move this rant on its way, let us note that ...analog media are not dead and gone. Indeed, it becomes increasingly clear that analog provides a deeper, richer, more satisfying media experience in many respects than what we usually find on screens.

To wit:

Print book sales are steadily rising year after year while ebook sales have been dwindling; so says the Association of American Publishers. A print book is an almost perfect thing. As Sax goes on to say: "People are buying books because a book engages nearly all the senses, from the smell of the paper and glue to the sight of the cover design and weight of the pages read, the sound of those sheets turning and even the subtle taste of the ink on your fingertips. A book can be bought and sold, given and received, and displayed on a shelf for anyone to see. It can start conversations and cultivate romances."

And what to make of the boom in vinyl record sales. In addition to the literally millions offered in vintage shops, there are, sources say, more than 200,000 newly pressed records sold each week! People say vinyl just sounds different: richer, softer, better. And it's not just nostalgia driven old folks; most of the sales are to young people.

Interestingly too, some professors are banning laptops, tablets, and even phones from classes and seminars. The research is unequivocal; college students learn less well when the employ laptops and tablets during lectures. Often students (if, indeed, they are on task at all) will merely type a lecture verbatim with little if any processing of the ideas. Notes taken with pen and paper, on the other hand, require students to follow the idea thread that the professor is teasing out and record summary notes—all of which require mental engagement. Harder, yes, but consistently shown by better comprehension and higher grades to be more useful.

And so on--

To conclude this rant, of course it's not a choice of one or the other: digital or analog. It's both at the same time (an analog concept). But the complexity of life and living is often best served with an equally complex awareness, one that honors our mammalian depth and diversity.

Speaking of black-and-white, were I working with photography, I would favor film and paper prints, preferably black and white. Analog delivers a richness of experience a depth—a sort of soul. To make a music trope—digital displays musical notes, but analog plays the music.

~ Bob Wood

Bob Wood, writer, artist, potter, historian, and volunteer extraordinaire, began his career as an artist following his retirement from teaching Language Arts. Bob serves as Studio B's gallery adjunct and invites the public for wide-ranging discussions on art, history, and the art and craft of writing. Bob has published four books on local history, contributes a weekly column to the area's local newspaper, is a popular speaker and presenter at local civic, service, and history organizations, and serves as President of the New Hanover Township Historical Society and board member and museum director of the Goschenhoppen Historians.

"Tamborine" art by Bob Wood

"Channeling Your Inner Baby" art by Jim Meehan

TONY THE LIP

was
older than he looked,

was
impressed
by the smell of his own farts,

lied
about everything,

never
held a job for long,

ate
everything,

drank
anything,

and
changed his shorts

once
a week.

Tony had
3 bad marriages,

4 shack-ups,

and
that one month he
never cared to talk about.

i rather liked
Tony.

~ John Yamrus

SHE

had
the gift
of recreational shallowness...

knew
how to be trivial...

and
how to avoid
emotional excess.

what
she didn't know...

what
she couldn't do...

was figure
a way past Tommy.

he
may have been creepy,

and
his smile
at times was blank...

but,
that tat of his...

that
god damn tattoo...

sure
looked sweet.

~ John Yamrus

Since 1970 John Yamrus has published 26 volumes of poetry, 2 novels and one volume of non-fiction. He has also had nearly 2,000 poems published in print magazines around the world. Selections of his poetry have been translated into several languages, including Spanish, Swedish, French, Japanese, Italian, Romanian, Albanian and Bengali. His poetry is regularly taught in colleges and universities. His newest book, MEMORY LANE, a memoir looking back at his childhood growing up in a Pennsylvania coal mining community, is a highly anticipated addition to his published work. His website is: <http://www.johnyamrus.com>

Artists' Biographies

Susan Biebuyck: Nourishing her own creative spirit, Susan Biebuyck has been an artist all her life. She majored in studio fine art at Kutztown University in Pennsylvania. She is known for her acrylic, oil, pastel and watercolor painting diversity, she calls herself "an art supplies junky" and works in a variety of media with fluency. Her work demonstrates superb observation and lyrical spirit, and has won honors and awards. She was an inaugural GoggleWorks studio artist in Reading, Pennsylvania.

Together in 2008, Susan & Jane founded Studio B, a non-profit, communityrun gallery, located in the heart of historic Boyertown, Pennsylvania. The gallery supports a healthy and thriving artists' membership. Susan has curated more than 100 exhibits to uphold Studio B's mission to promote art and artists from the local area. This is the 5th "Art Responding to Literature" and "Literature Responding to Art" book that Susan and Jane have put together.

Sue Ciccone: Nature is Sue's inspiration and her works are an emotional response to Creation. Whether it's the beauty of a landscape or the innocence of a creature, each subject she paints is the result of her life experiences. Sue's desire is for people see joy, peace and contentment in and through her art.

Sue DaNym: Quick to laugh and to comment on the petty and the profound, Sue is a literal artist. She likes to doodle and carries a pen and watercolor set in her purse. She often draws people when they are not looking. She once got sent to the principal's office for drawing her teacher in English class. That doodle was later hung in the school library where it still hangs today. Sue prefers not to have a studio but works in public, at cafes, stores, airports, parks, the street, etc. Sue is always drawing from life.

Tamie Dickson is an assistant professor and co-coordinator of developmental mathematics. Aside from teaching, she experiments with a variety of lenses, style, and post-editing software to enhance her skills and photos. She also collaborates with local author Catherine (Cat) Mahony, providing the photography for several of Cat's ekphrastic poems. Contact: tdickson@racc.edu

Kathi Ember is a professional illustrator and a political activist who is mad as hell. She has been a freelance illustrator for over 35 years with a focus on children's illustration for the past 20. www.kathiember.com

Adriano Farinella: Clouds have always been the symbol of impermanence for Adriano, constantly changing in service of and as a reaction to their environment. For Adriano, they are at once the beginning of things and the end of things, and painting them from memory and imagination is his way to cultivate the practice and art of paying attention and refine mindfulness. He sees the clouds to be like human figures—born, alive for a time, changing frequently, and then leaving. He is most inspired by paying attention to the present moment and to the evolution of memory and imagination.

Charley Farrell: Charley's work captures a person's inner self and reveals their strength or vulnerability, anxiety or serenity, arrogance or humility, their public self or their inner-life. In 1996, after 30 years Charley sold his architectural firm and pursued a Master of Fine Arts degree in painting. After graduation, he worked for two years as a Resident Affiliate Artist at the Tryon Center for Visual Arts and was represented by the Hodges Taylor Gallery, both located in Charlotte, North Carolina. His work received an award in a juried exhibition in the Art of the State of Pennsylvania. Several of his paintings were accepted by the North Carolina Museum of Art in a juried show of North Carolina artists. His artwork has been exhibited in New York, Pennsylvania, and North Carolina.

Angela Faust-Izzo: Angela's process begins with a laugh. She searches for humor and sarcasm in the things she observes, the people she knows, and the culture from which she comes. She uses humor as a vehicle to communicate how she feels and what she's thinking. Her hope is that all of her viewers are able to connect with the people that she paints and the humorous stories she tries to tell, regardless of their level of art appreciation.

Suzanne Fellows earned her BFA from Kutztown University and her MFA in Visual Arts from Vermont College of Fine Arts. She teaches at RACC and at the Goggleworks and has been a Goggleworks Studio artist since 2009. Currently she is working on two series: solar plate prints documenting the recent full and new moons and a study of the intricacies of abstract painting in acrylic. Suzanne is a Studio B member, Goggleworks studio artist, painter, printmaker, teacher, student of abstract design, happy to rant about a pet peeve. suzannefellows.com

Dan Gorman: After spending the majority of his career as a commercial artist for a local company, Gorman took a leap and starting exploring life as a professional fine artist. Dan was an inaugural studio artist at the GoggleWorks Center for the Arts, a volunteer tour guide of the building for visitors and student groups, and an assistant in gallery installations. Dan works in oil to create masterful still lifes and landscape paintings. His assemblages often provide humor and social commentary.

Kate Hamburger *is currently studying illustration at Maine College of Art in Portland, Maine. She received the Dean's scholarship to attend there and is enjoying her experience immensely. She loves living in Maine despite the snow and cold. She attended Parkland High School for two years but ended her high school career at The Charter Arts School in Bethlehem where she developed her skills and love of art. She had the opportunity to illustrate a children's book called <u>Color My World</u> about ice skating and won the Art Department award for excellence in the arts. Her future plans include study abroad and developing ideas for more children's books. When she is not working or drawing, she loves to take pictures, hike and visit the beach.*

Marta Herman *started writing poems after a totally life-changing month, experiencing the powerful nature of Southern Africa . . . powerful and pure, loving and cruel, always filled with infinite in mysteries. Upon returning, she developed a process of watercolor painting that helps to bring forth visions and thoughts from heart and mind. These, which she calls 'Mind Pictures,' are accompanied by humorous poems.*

Heather Lippincott-Foust *is a mixed media portrait artist determined not just to survive but to thrive! While she grew up sketching and creating, she didn't consider taking up art as a career until 2012 when she made the decision to pursue what she loved. She uses paint, paper, fabric, old books, antique chandeliers—whatever touches her fancy at the moment in creating her portraits. Heather has reached national audiences through feature articles about her in several issues of Stampington magazines and by teaching online classes. HeatherFoustart.com*

Barrie Maguire: *A 1960 Notre Dame graduate, Barrie has been an advertising Art Director, a Creative Director at Hallmark Cards, a writer, editorial Illustrator and a painter of Ireland. In 1997 he founded NewsArt.com, the first online source of op-ed illustrations for newspapers all across North America and the world.*

Jeanette May *is a photo-based artist using a critical, sometimes playful, approach to investigate representation itself. Early training as a painter is evident in her carefully arranged compositions and rich color palette. Her recent still life project, Tech Vanitas, embraces the anxiety surrounding technological obsolescence.*
www.JeanetteMay.com Instagram: @JeanetteMayArt

Challenges, Tempests, and Petty Annoyances   165

Ed McCarty *started his drawing and painting in earnest in 2005 when he retired from his career as a technical writer and illustrator. Largely self-taught using pen and ink and watercolor, Ed tries to maintain a realistic style even in his impressionistic works which feature his city, town, harbor, and landscape scenes and are inspired by a genuine appreciation of their historic or natural beauty.*

Jim Meehan *was born in Brooklyn, N.Y. in 1952. His father was an artist on New York newspapers. Jim graduated from Fordham University with a BS in Psychology and then attended the School of Visual Arts for two years. After art school he worked at the <u>New York Daily News</u> and in advertising. Jim has been printed in many publications and has participated in numerous group shows.*

Lynn Millar *has painted professionally for over 30 years and has exhibited in as far west as Kansas and as far east as New York City. Lynn is an award-winning artist and signature member of the Pennsylvania Watercolor Society, the Philadelphia Watercolor Society and the Baltimore Watercolor Society. In abstract and realism styles, Lynn's art is a constant exploration of her environment by color, design, texture and composition. In watercolors, she sometimes completes the painting with little or no brushwork, trying to control the paint with wetness, paper resists, or any other substance that affects the paint. The opaque mediums of acrylic, pastel, and casein allow a break from the planning and control needed with watercolor.*

Dave Nally *is a retired steel worker who likes to make art in his spare time. He sometimes goes by his nickname Big Dutch.*

Linda Rohrbach-Austerberry *is an artist, potter, and teacher. After first experiencing the fascination of working in clay as an art major at Indiana University of Pennsylvania, she made a lifetime commitment to the medium. She received both her B.S. in Art Education and M.A. in Ceramics from Indiana University of Pennsylvania. She taught Ceramics at the Boyertown Area Senior High School for 35 years.*

Mary Salen: *This series of protest signs were conceived and created for the 2017 Women's March on Washington by Mary Salen, with help from her husband, Stu. They were created as a response to the grotesque candidacy of our current president — and to answer it with the power of women.*

Matt Smith: As an interdisciplinary artist, Matt Smith works to create imagery structures that illustrate the transition from adolescence to adulthood. After completing a Bachelor's program in Photography and Design in 2014, Matt went on to continue his education in Kuldiga, Latvia, as a participant of the International Summer School of Photography Master Program under the tutelage of internationally acclaimed photographer Yurie Nagashima. From there, he has attended numerous workshops and residencies and is currently developing his own studio practice in book arts, mixed media, and sculptural work. Smith lives in Reading, Pennsylvania, and is an art instructor at Goggleworks Center for the Arts.

Erika Stearly is a lifelong resident of Pennsylvania, and a Kutztown University alum. Her paintings have been featured in both local venues and international gallery spaces, and she has taught for a few regional universities. More about Erika and her work can be found through a quick Google search of her name.

Theodore Thomas, retired engineering executive and Korean War veteran, traveled the world sketching, writing, and photographing his experiences over a working lifetime, drawing inspiration to create a body of pastel paintings that preserve his memories. Some have historical importance.

Naomi Vogels is an artist, a crafter, and a thinker who loves working with her hands. She is inspired by nature and family, and most recently influenced by viewing the world through the eyes of her young son. Her work continues to evolve, influenced by the muses of family and societal circumstances. She works in diverse artistic mediums—2D and 3D, including the creation of terrariums.

Reggie Waters is a visiting artist from Manchester, England. He is self-taught and enjoys painting classical subjects in a modern context.

Lauralynn White: An oil painter of landscapes and figures, Lauralynn fuses the human body with other forms found in the natural world, striving to illuminate the dark places of the psyche and celebrate the sacred nature of all things. Lauralynn's paintings express human emotion through organic forms, saturation of colour, and use of natural light. Much of her work relates to the current fragility of mankind and the environment. Lauralynn is a BFA graduate of Savannah College of Art and Design, an exhibiting member of the National Association of Women Artists, the Visual Arts in Chautauqua, and the current Gallery Director of GoggleWorks Center for the Arts, Reading, PA.

Bob Wood *always liked art, but has never taken an art class nor did it ever occur to him to make art himself until as an English teacher he modeled "risk taking" with his writing students and enjoyed liberal encouragement from his wife Sandra, an art teacher and artist. Bob is not trying to paint the way a thing looks, but render reality more forcefully and provide a shortcut to sensation. Bob uses house paint and some artist's acrylics on canvas to make his large pieces. He finds painting to be a struggle since he looks for help from chance and happy accident. Someone once described his paintings as "Basquait and Dubuffet crash into a Pennsylvania Dutch village." He likes that.*

Kristen Woodward: *received her BFA degree in Printmaking from Syracuse University and her MFA in Studio Art from Clemson University. Her mixed media works combine painting and printmaking and often utilize found collage materials. Woodward is currently a Professor of Art at Albright College teaching painting, printmaking, interdisciplinary courses on Latin American graphic art, and gender in the visual arts. Her own artworks are in numerous public collections.*

Jillian Wright-Prout *obtained a BFA from Kutztown University, studied under Myron Barnstone in Old Masters techniques. She loves to paint in watercolor, oils, and egg tempera. Jillian has been a proud member of Studio B since its inception. Her inspirations include Albrecht Durer, JMW Turner, Georgia OKeefe, N.C. Wyeth and Jamie Wyeth.*

The End

www.ingramcontent.com/pod-product-compliance
Lightning Source LLC
Chambersburg PA
CBHW032048150426
43194CB00006B/459